Cooking Up a Storm

Cooking Up a Storm

SYDNEY P. WAUD

Illustrations by Susan Tantlinger

Chatham Square Press, Inc.
New York, New York

Library of Congress Cataloging in Publication Data

Waud, Sydney P
   Cooking up a storm.

   Includes index.
   1. Cookery. I. Title.
TX715.W3473   641.5   77-10132
ISBN 0-89456-007-7

Book Design by Soho Studio

Published by Chatham Square Press
401 Broadway, New York, N.Y. 10013

Printing 123456789

Printed in the United States of America

Distributed by Contemporary Books, Inc.
180 North Michigan Avenue, Chicago, Ill. 60601

To I.M.B. whose spectacular
cooking stimulated my interest
in food beyond its consumption,
and to A.N.B., the proprietor
of "the best restaurant on the
Eastern Seaboard."

TABLE OF CONTENTS

A cookbook is like a gold mine: how many nuggets you find determines its value.

Anonymous

FOREWORD

Anybody who has a number of cookbooks usually singles out one as a favorite. However, the number of recipes actually used from that one book is very small in comparison to the total number of recipes contained therein. Mindful of this and the fact that most people seem to have neither the time nor the basic know-how for preparing food, I set out to produce a collection of some 180 recipes whose merits are based on a combination of practicality, simplicity and supreme taste. Many are old standards with some new or streamlined methods to facilitate overall preparation; others are refreshingly new and different.

It is rare today for a totally different, all-new recipe to be concocted. Consequently, contemporary cookbooks are usually made up of numerous theme variations of basic recipes. This book is an exception in that it gives one and only one recipe for preparing your favorite foods—like Roast Beef or Chewy Chocolate Chip Cookies—with the greatest of ease and the most success. In addition there are several not-so-well-known recipes—such as Bar B-Que Beef, Cock-A-Doodle-Doo or Shrimp Paradiso—any one of which could alone be worth the price of the book.

To add to the book's overall usefulness, handy reference sections have been included to cover such areas as weights and measures (including the metric system), cheeses, fruits and general culinary cues. It is these elements, coupled with simple and delicious recipes, which make this book distinctive and valuable to all who cook.

INTRODUCTION

From the outset all should be aware that I am neither an Escoffier nor a James Beard. My connection with food stems from an endless fascination with its preparation coupled with a love for consuming it. So understandably, I experience great discomfort when confronted by watery scrambled eggs, or once-green string beans now limp and pale yellow, or the classic cup of coffee which wakes you up only to kill you.

It is hard to believe this still happens when one considers that the 21st century is just around the corner. But the reason for it is simple. Many of us have not taken the small effort necessary to learn how to prepare even the most basic foods.

So I decided to try to correct this situation. Consequently, this book and its main purpose: to set down the simple, basic realities of food and its preparation, so that without expensive, single-purpose cooking equipment and exotic ingredients anyone who can read can prepare an excellent meal with a minimum of time, effort, and expense.

Another reason for the book is to present an abridged version of those voluminous cookbooks which are crammed with too many "fringe" recipes—variations for the sake of variation. With this book I want to narrow the choice to those recipes with the simplest preparation and the most delicious and honest results.

My ideas regarding food have always been very basic: (1) keep it simple and practical—the preparation of food should never be so tedious or demanding as to diminish the joy of eating and (2) keep the work load down and the taste factors up. This, of course, instantly rules out high-grade gastronomics— haute cuisine—which can be demanding to the point of delirium. Beside that, the equipment and training needed for this type of cookery puts it out of range for all but a very few people. (My advice to those who get an uncontrollable craving for haute cuisine is to treat yourself to a restaurant that has the chefs with the experience, time, utensils and clean-up squad. Such evasive

INTRODUCTION

action could prevent hari-kari which also takes a lot of time to clean up.)

In preparing a meal the ultimate goal is to preserve and intensify when possible the natural flavor of fresh ingredients. It is a matter of relying more on basic ingredients than complicated technique—that is the basis of culinary simplicity. Without question, when preparing food according to this theory, raw materials are of number one importance.

Success in combining good ingredients and simple technique to produce great meals is determined by a melange of the following: basic kitchen savvy; a "touch" or knack similar to playing the piano by ear; experience; and, of course, the ability to read and follow directions. Beyond the boundaries of applied knowledge and recipe reading is the limitless, wondrous world of creative cuisine. And what that takes is imagination, common sense, extra cents, inspiration, wasted groceries, a sense of humor, and 24-carat friends with candid opinions and strong stomachs.

Many of the recipes and libations contained in the book are old standards like roast beef and iced tea with slightly or completely different preparation suggestions which are geared to make old favorites easier to prepare and/or taste a whole lot better. There are also less familiar recipes which are either my own adaptations or hoarded secrets pried from recalcitrant house domestics, chefs, and friends (many of them Texans).

As an aside, I want to add a few comments on aphrodisiacs. For centuries people have been gulping an incredible variety of foods and concoctions which have been labelled aphrodisiacs, all purporting to have you busting box springs all over town. I hate to be a wet blanket, but it's all hogwash.

David R. Rubin devotes fourteen pages in his book to answering questions you were always afraid to ask concerning aphrodisiacs. He emphatically gives the hook to everything from

INTRODUCTION

powdered rhinoceros horn to ginseng and bivalves. There is only one potion which he feels can lay any claim to the tag of aphrodisiacs and that is alcohol—it works by simply diluting inhibitions. Another "authority" on this matter is that sensuous woman, "J". Like Rubin, she squashes just about every legend known regarding aphrodisiacs. What they both conclude is exactly in line with my thinking on the issue. "J" summed it up with: "Delicious foods, yes. Aphrodisiacs, no." To put some flesh on this theory, think back to Tom Jones and Mrs. Winter sucking down oysters, gnawing on mutton chops, quaffing lager, and mouthing pears. That's psychosexuality, not aphrodisia. It's the enticing smells drifting from savory morsels which send the senses reeling.

And so, the recipes in this book are not guaranteed to set senses ablaze or to make you a Galloping Gourmet. However, with reasonable success you may well attain the status of a semi-sensualist or a cantering culinarian.

WHAT TO EAT

In nearly all the local markets throughout this country there is always an enormous variety of food. Because the selection is so vast, it is hard to remember all the foods available when preparing a shopping list. This can lead to the syndrome of buying "the same old stuff" day after day. The following list is intended to help solve that problem by presenting the basic food choices by category. Some recipes have been included to provide a broader, more useful selection. An asterisk indicates that a preparation for that food or recipe appears in this book.

SOUPS
bean*
beef broth
bisque*
borscht
chicken*
chowder*
corn*
gazpacho*
gumbo
madrilene
minestrone
pea
tomato*
turtle
vegetable
vichyssoise*
watercress*

PASTA
fettucini*
macaroni*
noodles*
ravioli
spaghetti*
vermicelli

EGGS
Benedict*
french toast*
omelets*
quiche*
souffles*

SALADS
aspic*
avocado
Caesar*
celery*
chef 's*
coleslaw*
combination
cucumber*
endive
fruit
potato*
shrimp
spinach*
watercress

MEATS
bacon
baloney

barbecue beef*
boiled beef*
bratwurst
corned beef
frankfurters*
ham*
hamburger*
kidneys
knackwurst
lamb*
liver*
meat loaf*
pork*
pot roast*
salami
sausage
spareribs*
steak*
sweetbreads
tartare*
tongue
veal
venison

WHAT TO EAT

MISCELLANEOUS
casseroles*
chili*
fondue*
goulash
hominy
pizza
rarebit*
stew*

GAME AND POULTRY
chicken*
duck*
Cornish game hen*
goose*
pheasant*
quail*
squab*
turkey*

VEGETABLES
acorn squash*
artichoke*
asparagus*
baked beans*
beets*
bell pepper
broccoli*
Brussels sprouts*
cabbage*
(green and red)
carrots*
cauliflower*
celery
chayote*
(or mirliton)
corn*
cucumber

eggplant
kale
kidney beans
kohlrabi
lima beans
mushrooms*
okra
onions*
peas*
potato
pumpkin
radishes
rhubarb
rutabaga
sauerkraut
spinach*
string beans*
summer squash*
sunchoke
sweet potato*
tomato
turnips
winter squash*
zucchini*

FISH*
bass
bluefish
codfish
flounder
haddock
halibut
mackerel
pompano
red snapper
salmon
sole
swordfish
trout*

tunafish*

SHELLFISH
clams
crabs*
(hard- and soft-shell)
crawfish
lobster*
mussels
oysters
scallops*
shrimp*
steamer clams

DESSERTS
brownies
cake*
cheese*
cookies*
custard*
fruit*
fudge*
ice cream*
jello*
mousse*
pastry
pie*
pudding*
sherbet*
souffle*
zabaglione*

GENERAL INFORMATION REGARDING RECIPES

All ingredients are printed in bold letters.

Ingredients are listed in the order of their use in preparing a recipe.

Pre-preparation instructions such as washing, peeling, and chopping are given with the ingredient.

Substitutions like margarine for butter and stock for broth are not given but are perfectly acceptable unless otherwise specified. (Using fresh ingredients and freshly processed seasonings, i.e. freshly grated Parmesan cheese and ground pepper, will always produce better results.)

Salted water is made by adding 1 tablespoon salt to 1 quart water. (Cooking in salted water not only adds flavor to food but also helps keep it crisp. This occurs because salt adds bulk to water making it cook more efficiently without penetrating the food.)

Cooking times for bulky foods such as roasts are based on their being at or near room temperature (70°).

Where possible, preheating has been eliminated to reduce cooking time and energy consumption. (Remember that briefly opening the door of a hot oven can cause a 25° to 75° loss of heat.)

Soups

It has long been a custom to begin a formal or informal dining experience with soup. Indeed, there is something elegant and highly satisfying in serving a soup which has a delicate, refined flavor and proper consistency. Unhappily, many soups are so sophisticated and involved that to do them properly can be an exasperatingly difficult and time-consuming task, often out of proportion to the results. Happily, however, there are a number of delicious soups which can be made with a minimum of time and effort, and a maximum of imagination and innovation. Some of the following recipes are examples of that approach in full application.

CIN-CIN SOUP

Serves 4

2 cans (12-oz. size) **V-8 juice**
1 cup **dry vermouth**
1/4 teaspoon **salt**
2 teaspoons **fresh parsley**, chopped

Bring V-8 juice to boil. Separately heat the vermouth—*do not boil.*
Combine the two. Add salt and garnish each serving with parsley.

Nothing could be easier; it's also referred to as the Italian heartstarter.

NEW ENGLAND CLAM CHOWDER   Serves 4-6

1 quart **chowder clams** (with their broth*)
1 can (10 oz.) **potato soup**
2 tablespoons **butter**
1 teaspoon **salt**
1/2 teaspoon freshly **ground pepper**
1 medium **yellow onion**, chopped
1 tablespoon **bacon fat**
1 pint **light cream**

   *Often referred to as the liquor.

Drain clams saving the broth. Mince the clams. Put the broth, potato soup, butter, salt, and pepper in heavy pot and bring to boil. Meanwhile, saute onion in bacon fat for 3 minutes—do not brown. Add onion, light cream, and chopped clams to chowder. Heat to serving temperature being careful *not to boil*—clams get tough if overcooked.

The real thing with no great effort.

fair

CREAMY CORN SOUP   Serves 4

1 medium **yellow onion**, finely chopped
2 tablespoons **butter**
1 pint **milk***
1/2 teaspoon **salt**
1/4 teaspoon **pepper**
2 cans (17-oz. size) **cream-style corn**
Paprika

*For thicker consistency, use light or heavy cream.

In heavy saucepan saute onion in butter for 3 minutes—do not brown. Add milk, salt and pepper, and scald. Meanwhile, place corn in blender and mix at medium speed for 30 seconds. Stir into scalded milk and heat to serving temperature. Garnish with a dash of paprika on each serving.

This soup is superb hot or cold.

excellent

GAZPACHO
(Cold Tomato Soup)   **Serves 4-6**

1 clove **garlic**
1/4 cup **olive oil**
6 ripe **tomatoes**, peeled* and chopped
3/4 cup **green pepper**, finely chopped
2 **white onions**, finely chopped
1 medium **cucumber**, peeled and finely chopped
1 cup **tomato juice**
1/4 cup **red wine vinegar**
1/8 teaspoon **Tabasco sauce**
1 teaspoon **salt**
1/2 teaspoon freshly **ground pepper**
1 cup **croutons**

   *To peel tomatoes simply dunk them in boiling water for 25 seconds.

Mash garlic with a few drops of oil in the bottom of a large mixing bowl. Add remaining ingredients and stir well. Chill at least 1 1/2 hours before serving. Garnish each serving with croutons.

Alternate preparation (not as authentic, but much faster):

Place all the ingredients except onions in a blender for 20 seconds at medium speed. Stir in finely chopped onions and chill.

This dish of Spanish origin makes a great start for a warm weather meal.

LOBSTER BISQUE   Serves 4-6

1 medium **yellow onion**, peeled and quartered
1 stalk **celery**, chopped
1/2 teaspoon **marjoram**
1 quart **milk**
3 tablespoons **butter**
3 tablespoons **flour**
1 teaspoon **paprika**
3/4 teaspoon **salt**
1/3 teaspoon **white pepper**
1 cup **heavy cream**
2 tablespoons **dry sherry**
2 cans (6-oz. size) **lobster meat***, chopped

   *Any fish or shellfish can be substituted.

Place onion, celery, marjoram, and milk in a heavy saucepan and scald over low heat. In a separate saucepan melt butter, then stir in flour, paprika, salt, and pepper. Strain milk into sauce. Cook while stirring until it begins to thicken. Add lobster meat and cream. Over slow heat bring almost to boiling. Remove from heat and add sherry.

The cream improves both the taste and consistency of the soup. However, if diet is a consideration, it may be eliminated.

MELON PATCH SOUP   Serves 4-6

2 **cantaloupe melons**
1/2 cup **Half & Half**
1 cup **watermelon**, diced

Cut melon from rind taking care not to include any green-colored rind and discard seeds and fiber. Place melon in blender and mix at medium speed for 20 seconds. Strain and stir in Half & Half. Chill at least 1 hour before serving. Just before serving, garnish with diced watermelon.

A magnificent way to enjoy Cucumis Melo cantalupensis with Citrullus vulgaris—the latin names for cantaloupe and watermelon respectively.

SENEGALESE   Serves 4-6

2 cans (10-oz. size) **cream of chicken soup**, undiluted
1 pint **Half & Half**
1 1/4 cups **apple juice**
1/2 cup **dry white wine**
3/4 tablespoon **curry powder**
2 teaspoons **catsup**

Combine well all the ingredients. If too thick, add more Half & Half. Serve hot or chilled according to season or preference.

This recipe is a short-cut to a superb soup.

VICHYSSOISE   Serves 4-6

2 **baking potatoes**, peeled, washed and coarsely chopped
1 cup **leeks** (white part only), washed and chopped
1 pint **chicken broth**
1 cup **water**
3/4 teaspoon **salt**
1 cup **light cream**
1/4 teaspoon **white pepper**
2 tablespoons chopped **chives**

In heavy pot simmer potatoes, leeks, and salt in chicken broth
and water for 40 minutes. Then add light cream and pepper, and
force soup through a food mill or large strainer. Chill until very
cold—at least 1 hour. Garnish with chives.

Not as difficult as one might imagine. . . also very good hot.

WATERCRESS SOUP   Serves 4

1 bunch fresh **watercress**
1 quart (three 10-oz. cans) **chicken broth**
1 **scallion**, chopped
1/2 teaspoon **dill**
1/2 teaspoon **salt**
1 cup **light cream***

   *Milk or heavy cream may be substituted to alter taste and consistency.

Place all ingredients except light cream in a heavy pot and bring
to a boil. Remove from heat, cover and let stand 4 hours or
refrigerate overnight. Strain and add light cream. Serve hot—do
not boil—or chilled.

Always a crowd-pleaser and very easy.

ZUBBA-ZUBBA   Serves 6-8

1 quart (approx. three 10-oz. cans diluted with five cups water)
   black bean soup, chilled

Garnishes:
1 cup each:
   celery, chopped
   tomatoes, chopped
   croutons
   egg white (hard-boiled), chopped
   Mong bean sprouts (optional)
   alfalfa sprouts (optional)
1/2 cup each:
   parsley, chopped
   egg yolk (hard-boiled), chopped
2 or 3 tablespoons **lemon rind,** grated

Serve garnishings in separate bowls or from a condiment tray;
each person chooses the variety and quantity of garnishings
preferred.

*An excellent summer soup. Use as many of the suggested
garnishings as are available or suit your taste.*

Eggs, Cheese and Pasta

EGGS: Some 65 billion eggs are consumed in the USA every year. On their own or in combination with other foods and seasonings to make pancakes, pastas, sauces, meringues, souffles and more attesting to their usefulness and versatility.

CHEESES: Cheese is considered by many people as the ultimate in gastronomic pleasures. It is consumed in nearly all parts of the world and varies dramatically in taste, size and consistency. It is an integral part of many pasta dishes, casseroles and, of course, the almighty pizza. Eaten in combination with a compatible fruit, bread and beverage, cheese can in itself be a delicious meal (see page 195). When heated or cooked to make a fondue or soufflé, the full flavor of cheese reaches perfection.

PASTA: Italy is the country of origin for this wide variety of flour-and-egg based food. The dishes familiar to most people are spaghetti with a sauce and grated cheese and fettucini with a light cream sauce.

BAKED: (see SHIRRED)

BENEDICT: A soft-poached egg served on top of a toasted English muffin with a thin slice of baked ham and smothered with a delicate hollandaise sauce (page 125).

Not especially thinning and a little time-consuming to prepare, but every once in a while well worth the calories and the effort.

BOILED: *Soft-cooked*—submerge eggs in boiling water for approximately 3 1/2 minutes.

Hard-cooked — Cold-water method: place eggs in saucepan and add enough water to cover. Place over heat. When water is at full boil, remove from heat. Cover and let eggs stand in water for 15 minutes. Then run cold water over eggs and refrigerate 45 minutes.

Boiling-water method: submerge eggs in boiling water for 20 minutes. (To make yolks set in the middle, use a spoon to turn them for the first minute.) When eggs are cooked, dunk them in cold water. Refrigerate 45 minutes before using.

To prevent eggs from cracking, they should be at room temperature when placed in boiling water. If eggs are cold, a small pinprick in the round end prevents cracking.

CODDLED: Grease coddling cup (or individual baking dish with butter. Add seasoning of your choice (cheese, shallots, salt, pepper, etc.). Then crack egg into cup taking care not to break yolk. Add more seasoning if desired. Secure top on cup. Place in 2" of simmering water for 8 to 10 minutes for soft cooked—adjust time for harder cooked eggs.

CURRIED: Serves 4

2 tablespoons **butter**
1 1/2 tablespoons **flour**
1 1/2 teaspoons **curry powder**
1 teaspoon **instant onion** (optional)
1/2 teaspoon **salt**
1/4 teaspoon **pepper or cayenne**
1/4 cup **chicken broth**
1/2 cup **milk** or **light cream**
8 **hard-boiled eggs**, sliced

In double boiler melt butter. Stir in flour and cook over direct, low heat for 2 to 3 minutes—do not brown. Add curry, onion, salt and pepper. Slowly blend in broth and milk. When sauce is smooth, add sliced eggs and place over simmering water for about 15 minutes. Serve on toasted bread or English muffin.

FRIED: *Sunnyside-up*—Melt 1 tablespoon butter or margarine in frying pan over medium-high heat. When butter begins to bubble, crack eggs into pan and fry 3 to 4 minutes. (To cook yolk, turn egg and fry for 10 to 15 seconds.)

Water-fried* — Place 2 teaspoons butter or margarine in frying pan over medium-high heat. When butter begins to bubble, crack eggs into pan and fry 1 to 2 minutes. Add 1 tablespoon water to bottom of pan and cover tightly. Cook 1 to 2 more minutes.

*This combination of poaching and frying produces a very delicate, almost elegant egg.

OMELET: *Plain* or *seasoned*—Beat 2 eggs, 1/8 teaspoon salt, a dash of pepper, and 1 tablespoon water or milk until well combined. Place omelet pan or heavy skillet over medium heat. Melt 1 tablespoon butter to sizzling—do not burn. Pour egg mixture into pan. Add desired seasoning (grated cheese, herbs, jelly, mushrooms, bacon, shallots, etc.) or leave plain. Slowly stir with fork and gently shake pan until eggs begin to set. When eggs are set but still slightly moist, quickly but gently fold end over with spatula and slide omelet onto a heated plate.

EGGS

POACHED: Put about 3/4" of water in shallow skillet. Bring to boil and add 1/2 teaspoon salt and 1 teaspoon vinegar. (This will help keep the egg white together and will not change the egg's flavor.) Carefully crack egg into water. Cover skillet, remove from heat and let stand 2 to 3 minutes or until white is firm. Remove egg from water with slotted spoon and allow to drain completely. Serve on toasted English muffin or on plain toast. (Eggs may also be poached in broth or milk according to taste preference.)

SCRAMBLED: Melt 1 tablespoon butter in skillet over medium-low heat. Beat together 2 eggs, a dash each of salt and pepper, 1 tablespoon light cream (optional) and any other desired seasoning. Pour into skillet. When eggs begin to thicken, stir gently with fork. When eggs have thickened but are still moist, remove from heat and serve.

SHIRRED (Baked): Preheat oven to 325°. Grease individual baking dish or ramekin. Carefully break 2 eggs into dish. Add 1 tablespoon light cream and 2 teaspoons melted butter. Season with salt and pepper to taste and sprinkle with parsley and/or grated cheese. Bake 10 to 12 minutes or to desired doneness.

SOUFFLÉ: In truth, preparing soufflés is not difficult. There are some simple basics which must be carefully followed, but beyond

that it is merely a matter of practice making perfect. The basics are:
- before preparation, thoroughly wash all utensils
- egg whites and yolks should be at room temperature (70°)
- always use a straight-sided casserole dish no larger than 2 quarts
- the size of the casserole dish must be correct relative to the amount of soufflé being made
- measurements must be exact
- to get higher soufflés make a "trench" in the soufflé mixture about 1″ deep 1″ from the edge of the casserole.
- cooking temperature must be constant
- avoid opening oven door until soufflé is done
- serve immediately on warmed plates

FRENCH TOAST   Serves 2

2 tablespoons **butter**
2 **eggs**, beaten slightly
1/8 teaspoon **nutmeg**
1/4 cup **light cream**
6 slices **white bread**, crust removed

Melt butter in skillet. Meanwhile, combine eggs, nutmeg, and
cream in mixing bowl. Dip bread slices into the mixture. For
each serving, stack together 3 slices of bread in skillet. Cover
and cook 7 to 8 minutes over medium-low heat. Flip and cook
covered 5 more minutes, or until lightly browned. Serve with
heated maple syrup.

A superior version of an old standard, discovered in Barbados.

CHEESE FONDUE   Serves 4

1 clove **garlic**
1 1/2 cups **dry white wine**
1 tablespoon **cornstarch** or 2 tablespoons **flour**
2 pounds **Swiss cheese** (Emmenthaler or Gruyere)*, grated
1 ounce **kirsch**** (optional)
2 loaves **Italian** or **French bread**, cut in 1" pieces so each piece has
  crust

*Use only imported brands, as domestic cheeses have less body and
tend to separate easily. Gruyere is stronger and more flavorful than
Emmenthaler.
**Use only good imported brand or substitute rum, cognac or applejack.

Rub interior of fondue pot with garlic. Combine wine and
cornstarch, and pour into pot. Place over medium-low heat
taking care not to boil. When hot, start adding cheese, stirring
constantly with wooden spoon. When all the cheese is melted,
continue to heat, stirring constantly until mixture becomes
smooth and creamy. Just before boiling, add the kirsch. Place on
fondue rack and adjust heat so fondue is slowly bubbling. To
eat, place bread cubes on fork and dunk into fondue.

*An authentic dish which was kindly given to me by the Swiss
culinary expert, Felix Meirer. Take care not to burn your mouth
as melted cheese retains a lot of heat.*

CHEESE AND BACON QUICHE
Serves 4

Single 9″ **pastry shell** (page 154)
1 cup **Swiss cheese**, coarsely grated
1/4 cup **Parmesan cheese**, freshly grated
4 **eggs**, slightly beaten
1 cup **light cream**
1 small **onion**, chopped
4 slices **bacon**, cooked crisp and crumbled
1 tablespoon **parsley**, finely chopped
Dash of **nutmeg** and **cayenne**

Pie crust — Set pastry into greased 9″ pie plate. Bake on center rack of oven at 400° for 10 minutes.

Filling — Set oven to 350°. Combine all ingredients and pour into pie shell to within 1/8″ of the top. Bake for 30 minutes or until custard is set and nicely browned. Let stand 5 minutes before serving.

This is a real delight when served with a crisp salad and wine.

WELSH RAREBIT   Serves 4

2 tablespoons **butter**
3/4 pound **sharp cheddar cheese**, grated
1 teaspoon **dry mustard**
1 teaspoon **Worcestershire sauce**
1/4 teaspoon **cayenne**
6 ounces **ale** *or* **lager beer**
2 **eggs**, slightly beaten
4 slices **toast**

Melt butter in double boiler. Add cheese, seasoning and ale.
When cheese has melted, add eggs and cook stirring constantly
until mixture is creamy and smooth. (If mixture curdles, put in
blender at high speed for 20 to 30 seconds.) Pour over toast and
serve.

*A delicious quickie too often forgotten. Leftovers of this meal-in-
itself will keep for about a week if refrigerated.*

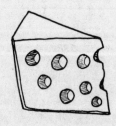

CHEESE SOUFFLÉ   Serves 4

3 tablespoons **butter**
4 tablespoons **flour**
1 1/2 cups whole **milk**
5 **egg yolks**, at room temperature
1 cup **cheddar cheese***, grated
1 teaspoon **dry mustard**
Dash each **nutmeg** and **cayenne**
3/4 teaspoon **salt**
1/8 teaspoon **cream of tartar**
7 **egg whites**, at room temperature
Grated **Parmesan cheese**

*Other cheeses may be substituted or use undiluted cheddar cheese soup.

Preheat oven to 400°. In large saucepan melt butter and blend in flour. Cook over low heat 3 minutes—do not brown. Remove from heat and gradually whisk in milk. Return to medium heat and stir in cheese, mustard, nutmeg, cayenne, and salt. Then add egg yolks one at a time whisking rapidly until mixture is thick and smooth. Remove from heat. Add tartar to egg whites and beat until stiff. Gently fold into soufflé base. Butter a 2-quart soufflé dish and sprinkle Parmesan over bottom and sides; invest dish and gently tap sides to remove excess cheese. Pour batter into dish—do not fill more than 3/4 full. Reduce heat to 375° and bake soufflé 30 to 35 minutes on middle rack of oven or until puffed high and lightly browned. Avoid opening oven door while soufflé is cooking.

FETTUCINE NICOLA   Serves 4-6

1/2 pound **sweet butter**
1 cup **heavy cream**
2 cups **Parmesan cheese**, freshly grated
1 pound **fettucine** or **egg noodles**, boiled al dente*
2 **egg yolks**
Black pepper, freshly ground

   *To cook pasta al dente means to boil until *just* tender—overcooking
will make pasta mushy.

Melt butter in large, heavy pot. Blend in cream and half the
cheese. Bring just to a boil. Add boiled noodles and stir. Remove
from heat. Add yolks and remaining cheese. Stir to mix
thoroughly. Give a few turns of a pepper mill over each serving.

Alternative: To make CARBONARA, add to the above recipe
1/2 pound prosciutto, pancetta,* or lean bacon, chopped and
fried almost crisp in 1 tablespoon olive oil.

*Pancetta makes a better dish, but is hard to find.

Fettucine is the Italian word for a certain size egg noodle.

SPAGHETTI   Serves 4

4 to 5 quarts **water**
4 tablespoons **salt**
1 tablespoon **olive oil**
1 package (1 pound) **spaghetti**

Bring water to rolling boil. Add salt, oil and spaghetti. Cook, uncovered, until limp—usually 7 to 9 minutes; stir occasionally to prevent sticking. Drain in colander—do not rinse—and immediately place in warm serving bowl.

Linguini and macaroni can be cooked the same as above. To complement your favorite pastas, try a delicious sauce (page 128) along with lots of freshly grated Parmesan cheese.

Meats

Cooking meats to perfection can be tricky due to a number of important factors such as: weight or thickness; whether the meat is frozen, chilled or at room temperature; if there is a bone or not; and the grade of meat. However, if all factors are adjusted for, success is inevitable. The following suggestions will help in getting the best results with meats.

FREEZING: 1 — Meat should be kept frozen at temperatures of zero or below. 2 — Chopped beef can be kept frozen 2 or 3 months while steaks and roasts can be kept 8 months to 1 year. 3 — Contrary to widespread belief, refreezing meat is safe as long as it is kept properly refrigerated in the interim. However, needless refreezing should be avoided.

DEFROSTING: If time permits, allow meat to defrost 24 hours under refrigeration. Otherwise, thaw at room temperature for 4 to 6 hours. Never unwrap meat during thawing and never thaw in water.

COOKING: 1 — Preheat broiler 10 to 15 minutes before using. 2 — Place meat 3 to 4 inches from heat source. 3 — Never puncture meat while cooking, otherwise it will lose some of its natural juices. 4 — Always let broiled, grilled, or roasted meat stand covered 10 to 15 minutes before carving. This allows juices to distribute evenly throughout the meat.

WESTERN BAR B-QUE BEEF   Serves 8

The word barbecue could stem from one of two sources: the Spanish word "barbacoa" which came from the Indian word for the wooden frame on which meat and fish were cooked; or the French who explained the Indian's outdoor pit-cooking of whole animals as "barbe à queue" or literally "beard to tail."

6-8 pound cut of **brisket, rump, round, or chuck**
8 **hamburger buns**

Marinade:
1/2 cup **vegetable oil**
1/4 cup **vinegar**
1 clove **garlic**, chopped
1/2 cup **dry sherry**
2 tablespoons **Worcestershire sauce**
1 teaspoon each **ground pepper** and **salt**

Place meat and marinade in plastic bag. Tie securely, put on platter and refrigerate 1 day. Remove meat and marinade from bag; drain off marinade and retain. Put meat in shallow baking pan lined with foil. Place on top shelf of cold oven and set heat to 325°. Roast 4 hours or until tender; baste with marinade every 30 minutes turning the meat once. Slice cross-grain and serve on heated hamburger buns with lots of Bar B-Que sauce (page 118).

This recipe demands some attention because of the basting, but produces barbecue beef at its best. Serve with lots of crisp salad and cold beer.

BREWED HOT DOGS   Serves 6

12 all-beef **hot dogs**
1 can or bottle (12 oz.) **light beer**
1 cup **water**
2 **bay leaves**
6 **peppercorns**

Put all the ingredients in a saucepan. Bring to a boil, adjust heat
to a slow simmer, cover and cook 15 to 20 minutes.
Served traditionally with warmed hot dog buns, mustards, and
relishes.

*Steaming frankfurters in beer gives an extra-special flavor to this
almighty American version of the wienerwurst. A quick roasting
on the barbecue adds the final traditional touch.*

HAMBURGER

Serves 4

1 1/3 pounds **ground chuck** *or* **round***
Salt and **pepper**
2 tablespoons **butter**
1 teaspoon **oil**
   *Best results are always obtained with beef which is freshly ground.

Form meat into patties and season with salt and pepper to taste. Broil or grill to preferred doneness. If pan-broiling, melt butter with oil in heavy skillet over medium-high heat. Add meat when butter begins to bubble. Cook to desired doneness—about 5 minutes on both sides for medium-rare. Traditionally served with hamburger buns, catsup or mustard, relish and sliced raw or fried onions (page 93).

Cheeseburger: Before meat is done, place 1 slice American or any other cheese on top of each hamburger and cover if pan-broiling or grilling, or place meat under broiler until cheese has melted.

Crunchy crust: Wipe both sides of hamburger with oil and/or soft butter and cook with high heat.

Recent statistics from the Department of Agriculture show that approximately 8 billion pounds of hamburger meat are consumed annually in the USA. That comes out to about 25 billion individual hamburgers.

CAROLINA BAKED HAM   Serves 10-12

6-7 pound pre-cooked shank end of **ham** (with bone), skinned*
1 cup **orange juice**
1 pint **ginger ale**
Water
10 **cloves**
3 tablespoons **brown sugar**
1/4 cup **prepared mustard**
1 cup **pineapple juice**

*If not done, ask your butcher to do this or to show you how.

Place ham in large kettle. Add orange juice, ginger ale, and
enough water to cover. Bring to simmer and cook for 1 hour.
Drain. Cut diamond pattern in fat and insert cloves. Combine
brown sugar and mustard, and spread over meat. Put ham fat
side up in baking pan lined with foil. Add pineapple juice to pan.
Place in oven, set heat to 325° and cook 1 1/4 hours, basting
twice. Allow ham to stand 10 minutes before carving. Hot or
cold ham is traditionally served with an assortment of mustards.

An easy favorite that goes a long way with a hungry crowd.

PERFECT ROAST BEEF   Allow 1 rib for 3 persons

Roast prime ribs of beef—3 ribs or larger
1 tablespoon **rosemary**, crushed
1/2 cup **flour**
2 tablespoons **salt**
2 teaspoons freshly **ground pepper**
1 cup **water**

Thoroughly rub all surfaces of roast with combined rosemary, flour, salt, and pepper. Place roast standing on ribs in shallow baking pan and add water. Place on center rack of oven. Turn oven to 375°—*do not preheat*. After required time for first heat has elapsed (rare: 1 hr. 30 mins.; medium-rare: 1 hr. 40 mins.; medium: 1 hr. 50 mins.), turn oven off. Leave roast in oven, but *do not open oven door*. One hour before serving, turn oven to 300°; it is important to allow at least 2 hours before the second heat.

Note: A great idiosyncrasy of this recipe is that roasts of 3 ribs or larger will cook to desired doneness with the same cooking time. An even bigger plus is that the meat cooks uniformly throughout.

This recipe is very convenient for the chef who must be away from the oven either to work or shop. Simply apply the first heat before leaving in the morning.

If onions and potatoes are to accompany the roast, parboil to fork tender, roll in pan drippings and place around roast prior to starting the second heat.

BOILED BEEF   Serves 6

4 pound **brisket** (cross rib)
Cold **water**
3 medium **yellow onions**, halved
12 **cloves** (stick into onions)
2 **carrots**, halved
8 **peppercorns**
1 teaspoon **dill**
1 **bay leaf**
2 teaspoons **salt**

Place brisket in large pot and add just enough water to cover.
Slowly bring to a boil. Adjust heat to attain a slow simmer. Cook
uncovered, skimming frequently. When scum ceases to form,
add remaining ingredients. Cover tightly and maintain slow
simmer for about 3 hours or until meat is very tender. Serve hot
or chilled according to season or preference.

*The simplicity of this dish belies its greatness. A popular
addition to this dish is horseradish sauce (page 126).*

BROILED LAMB CHOPS   Serves 4

8 **lamb chops**, 1 1/2″ to 2″ thick
1 tablespoon **rosemary**, crushed
2 teaspoons each **salt** and **pepper**
1/4 cup **butter**, melted

Preheat broiler. Sprinkle chops with rosemary, salt, and pepper.
Place them on a wire rack in a shallow baking pan lined with foil.
Broil 8 minutes. Turn chops, baste with butter and broil 6 more
minutes for medium-rare; adjust time for rare or medium.

*A delicious meat which is perfectly complemented with mint
sauce (page 127).*

BUTTERFLY LAMB

Serves 6-8

1 leg of **lamb** (5-6 pounds), boned*
1 clove **garlic**, cut in slivers
1 cup **dry red wine**
1 tablespoon **rosemary**
3 tablespoons **oil**
2 tablespoons **Worcestershire sauce**
1 teaspoon **salt**
3/4 teaspoon **pepper**

*When ordering meat, ask the butcher to remove the bone from a leg of lamb; the meat stripped from the bone in one piece and laid open roughly resembles a butterfly.

Make several 1/4" cuts in meat and insert slivers of garlic. Spread remaining ingredients over both sides of meat. Cover and let marinate 3 hours at room temperature. Grill, broil or pan-broil as a steak of the same size—about 12 to 14 minutes on both sides for medium rare. After cooking, cover and let stand 10 minutes before serving. Carve like a steak.

A superior way to prepare lamb which has gained popularity only in the past five years.

ROAST LEG OF LAMB   Serves 6-8

1 **leg of lamb** (5-6 lbs.)
1 clove **garlic**, cut in slivers
1 tablespoon **salt**
2 teaspoons **pepper**
1 tablespoon **rosemary**
1/2 cup **water**

On fatty side of lamb make several 1/4" cuts and insert slivers of garlic. Thoroughly rub all surfaces of lamb with combined salt, pepper, and rosemary. Place lamb on rack, fat side up, in shallow baking pan lined with foil. Add water to bottom of pan. To cook, follow one of the methods below:

One-heat method: Preheat oven to 500°. Roast on middle shelf of oven for 20 minutes. Reduce heat to 375° and continue roasting as follows: rare—40-45 mins.; medium-rare—50-55 mins.; medium—60-65 mins.

Two-heat method: Place roast on middle shelf of oven. Turn oven to 350°—do not preheat. After time for the first heat has elapsed (rare—1 hr. 15 mins.; medium-rare—1 hr. 25 mins.; medium—1 hr. 35 mins.), turn oven off. Leave roast in oven—*do not open oven door.* One hour before serving, turn oven to 300°. It is important to allow at least 2 hours before starting second heat.

Roast lamb is an elegant meal and certainly not difficult to prepare properly. Traditionally served with mint jelly or mint sauce (page 127).

CLASSIC STEAK TARTAR

Serves 2

1 teaspoon **Dijon mustard**
1/4 teaspoon each **salt** and **ground pepper**
1 1/4 tablespoons **oil**
1/2 teaspoon **wine vinegar**
1 **egg yolk**
1/8 teaspoon **Worcestershire sauce**
1 pound lean freshly **ground round** or **sirloin***
1 small **onion**, finely chopped
1 teaspoon **parsley**, chopped
3/4 tablespoon **capers**
1 loaf **pumpernickel bread**

*The shorter the time between when the meat is ground and when it is served, the better the taste.

Combine the mustard, salt, and pepper. Beat in the oil, vinegar, egg yolk, and Worcestershire sauce. Add the meat and mix well, using two forks. Add onions, parsley, and capers, and mix. Mold into desired shape and refrigerate 2 to 3 hours. Serve on chilled platter with pumpernickel bread.

Aside from being a great main dish, this recipe can also be served as a popular hors d'oeuvres on bread squares.

PEPPERED STEAK   Serves 6

3 pound **sirloin steak**,* about 1 3/4" thick
2 tablespoons **freshly cracked pepper**
1 1/2 ounces **cognac**, warmed

*If individual steaks are used, simply adjust cooking time.

Press pepper into both sides of meat. Cover and let stand 2
hours at room temperature. Pan-broil or broil to desired
doneness—about 7 minutes on both sides for medium-rare. Add
cognac and carefully ignite. When flame is out, remove steaks to
a heated platter and cover.

Sauce:
4 tablespoons **butter**
1 1/2 tablespoons **flour**
1/2 teaspoon **salt**
1 teaspoon **freshly cracked pepper**
1 teaspoon **Dijon mustard**
1 can (10 oz.) **beef broth**
1/2 cup **water**

Pour off all but 2 tablespoons pan drippings. Stir in butter, flour,
salt, and pepper. Place over medium heat and cook 3 minutes.
Remove from heat. Add the mustard and then slowly stir in
broth and water. Return to heat and reduce until sauce is
smooth. Pour sauce over steak or serve separately.

*Flaming food can be dangerous so be careful when making this
tasty version of steak au poivre.*

SPARERIBS

Serves 4

4 pounds **lean spareribs**

Plain and crispy: Place ribs in roasting pan lined with foil. Add 3/4 cup water. Put in cold oven and set heat to 400°. Bake, uncovered, 2 hours. Turn twice.

With barbecue sauce: Place ribs in roasting pan lined with foil. Add 3/4 cup water. Put in cold oven and set heat to 400°. Bake loosely covered with foil for 45 minutes without basting. Pour off fat. Reduce heat to 325° and cook, uncovered, 1 1/2 hours turning twice. Baste every 20 minutes with the following sauce:

1/2 cup **catsup or tomato sauce**
1/3 cup **cider vinegar**
1/2 cup **beef broth**
3/4 teaspoon **ground ginger**
1/2 teaspoon **pepper**

Place all ingredients in bowl and mix well.

One of the all-time great finger foods which doubles as either an appetizer or main course.

ROAST LOIN OF PORK   Serves 6

4-5 pound **boneless loin of pork**
3 tablespoons **flour**
1 tablespoon **salt**
2 teaspoons **pepper**
1 teaspoon **sage**
3/4 teaspoon **marjoram**
1 clove **garlic**, chopped
1/2 cup **apple cider**
1 cup **beef broth**

Rub meat with combined flour, salt, pepper, sage, and marjoram. Place on wire rack in roasting pan lined with foil. Add garlic, cider, and broth.

One-heat method: Preheat oven to 425°. Bake 30 minutes. Reduce heat to 325° and bake 1 hour and 20 minutes. Baste occasionally, adding more broth if needed. Let roast stand, covered, 10 minutes before carving.

Two-heat method: Without preheating, roast in 425° oven for 1 hour. Turn oven off leaving roast inside—*do not open oven door*. Fifty minutes before serving, turn oven to 300°. Allow at least 2 hours before second heat.

Note: Never undercook pork. The above cooking times are for a medium roast.

Pan sauce:
2 tablespoons **flour**
1 teaspoon **Dijon mustard**
1 1/2 tablespoons **catsup**
1 cup **applesauce**
2 teaspoons **horseradish**
1 cup **beef broth**
1 cup **water**

Spoon off excess grease. Stir in flour and cook over medium heat for 3 minutes. Add remaining ingredients. Remove from heat and add:

1 ounce **Calvados or apple jack** (optional)

A magnificent pork dish with not too much effort.

POT ROAST   Serves 8-10

2 tablespoons **oil**
3-5 pound **beef rump, bottom round,** *or* **brisket,** rolled*
1 tablespoon **Worcestershire sauce**
1 can (10 oz.) **tomato soup,** undiluted
1 can (8 oz.) **tomato sauce**
1/4 cup boiling **water**
1 tablespoon **vinegar**
2 medium **yellow onions,** sliced
Salt and **pepper**

*Ask your butcher to roll and tie the meat or ask him to show you how it's done.

Put oil in heavy kettle or Dutch oven. Add meat and brown on all sides over high heat. Remove from heat. Combine remaining ingredients, seasoning with salt and pepper to taste and pour over meat. Put in cold oven, set heat to 325° and roast, covered, 3 1/4 hours or until meat is tender. Remove meat to warmed serving platter. Degrease pan drippings and pour remaining sauce over meat.

Not very quick, but easy.

MEAT LOAF   **Serves 8-10**

3 slices **stale bread**, trimmed and crumbled
2 tablespoons **butter**, melted
3/4 cup **milk**
2 1/2 pounds **beef chuck**, freshly ground*
1 1/2 pounds fresh **pork**, ground
1/2 pound **sausage**, ground
1 large **onion**, finely chopped
2 **eggs**, slightly beaten
2 teaspoons **prepared mustard**
1/2 teaspoon **savory** or **tarragon**
1/2 teaspoon **oregano**
1 1/2 teaspoons **salt**
3/4 teaspoon **pepper**

*To simplify the job of mixing the meats, ask your butcher to grind them together for you.

Line shallow baking pan with foil and grease thoroughly. Combine bread, butter, and milk in large bowl. Add remaining ingredients and mix thoroughly with two forks. Moisten hands and shape mixture into a loaf. Place in baking pan. Put in cold oven, set heat at 375°, and bake 1 1/4 hours.

Alternatives: Bake in greased ring mold. Also try basting with catsup or chili sauce.

Remember that leftover meat loaf served chilled makes an excellent addition to any warm-weather meal.

MEAT BALLS   Makes about 12

1 pound **ground chuck beef**
1 clove **garlic**, minced
1 teaspoon **salt**
3/4 teaspoon **pepper**
1 slice **white bread**, trimmed and cut in small pieces
1/4 cup **milk, bouillon,** or **red wine**
1 **egg**, slightly beaten
Flour
3 tablespoons **oil**

Combine beef with minced garlic, salt, and pepper. Soak bread in milk. Squeeze most of liquid from the bread. Add the bread and egg to the meat and mix well. Form into balls and dust lightly with flour. Fry evenly in oil over medium heat for about 5 minutes.

Little effort for a big extra to serve with your favorite pasta dishes.

SAUTÉED CALF'S LIVER

**Serves 4
(allow two pieces
per person)**

4 slices **bacon**
1/2 cup **flour**
2 teaspoons **salt**
1 teaspoon **pepper**
1 1/4 pound **calf's liver**, cut in 1/4″ slices
4 tablespoons **butter**
1 cup **chicken broth**
2 teaspoons fresh **lemon juice**

Fry bacon until crisp in a large, heavy skillet; remove bacon to paper and drain. Pour off all but 2 tablespoons bacon drippings. Combine flour, salt, and pepper, and lightly dust liver slices. Add 2 tablespoons butter to skillet and melt over medium-high heat. When butter stops bubbling, sauté liver, allowing about 1 1/2 minutes per side. Remove meat to a heated platter or plates. Add chicken broth to skillet and reduce over high heat to about 3/4 cup. Remove from heat and stir in lemon juice and remaining butter. Pour sauce over liver and garnish with bacon.

For those who love liver, this is the recipe that does it to perfection.

Game and Poultry

Game, whether domestic or taken wild by the hunter, is always a special treat. Chicken—which is generally less expensive than meat, and certainly easy to prepare—is a delicious standard whether fried or fricasseed. And, of course, there is turkey, that indigenous bird which traditionally finds its way to the table for Thanksgiving and other holidays, but is economical and suitable for any time of the year; for a real change, try it barbecued.

Broiler: a young chicken weighing between 1 1/2 to 3 1/2 pounds.

Fryer or broiler-fryer: a broiler usually weighing over 2 1/2 pounds.

Roaster: a tender chicken weighing between 3 1/2 to 5 pounds.

Capon: a male chicken weighing between 4 to 8 pounds which has been desexed, resulting in a tender bird with a large amount of white meat.

Stewing: a mature female broiler or egg-layer.

ROAST TURKEY   Serves 10-12

10-12 pound **turkey**, washed and dried
6 tablespoons **butter**, melted
1 1/2 cups **chicken broth**
Salt and **pepper**
12 ounces **stuffing**, (page 51)

Brush butter over bird and lightly salt and pepper cavity and exterior. Stuff cavity 3/4's full and truss. (Do not stuff bird until ready to roast.) Put bird in roasting pan lined with foil. Add broth to pan. Place in cold oven and set heat to 350°. Cook 1 1/2 hours basting occasionally with butter. Cover bird and cook 2 more hours, basting every 30 minutes with pan juices. Remove cover and continue cooking until turkey has been roasted a total of 25 minutes per pound. Remove from oven, cover and let stand 20 minutes before carving.

Caution: Stuffing can spoil easily and contaminate the turkey. Therefore, always remove all remaining stuffing from the cavity when keeping leftover turkey for any length of time.

This festive bird requires a little attention while cooking but always proves well worth the effort.

ROCK CORNISH GAME HEN   Serves 4

4 **Rock Cornish game hens,** * washed and trussed
1/2 cup **chicken broth**
1/4 cup **dry white wine** or **vermouth**
1/4 cup **butter**, melted
Salt and **pepper**

*Preferably fresh.

Preheat oven to 475°. Line shallow roasting pan with foil—grease
the foil. Put birds in pan and pour broth and wine over them.
Sprinkle lightly with salt and pepper. Place pan in oven and
reduce heat to 350°. Roast 1 hour if stuffed (page 51) and
45 minutes if unstuffed, basting twice with butter. Put under
broiler for 2 or 3 minutes to brown. Let stand, covered, for
10 minutes. Pour pan juices over top and serve.

*A bird rarely thought of despite the fact it is widely available. This
recipe is also perfect for preparing squab—a bird not too often
available, but which makes a very elegant meal for a special
occasion.*

SOUTHERN FRIED CHICKEN   Serves 4

2 **fryer chickens**, quartered and washed
1/2 cup **oil**
1/4 pound (1 stick) **butter**
1 cup **self-rising flour**
1 tablespoon **baking powder**
1 teaspoon each **salt** and **pepper**
1/4 teaspoon **cayenne** (optional)

Submerge chickens in salted ice water (1 tablespoon salt to
1 quart water) and let stand 2 hours or overnight if possible.
Drain chickens and place on towel to dry. Put oil and butter in
large, heavy skillet and place over medium-high heat. Meanwhile,
dredge chicken with combined flour, baking powder, salt, and
pepper. Place chicken in hot oil—but not smoking—and cover.
Fry 5 minutes, remove cover and cook 10 more minutes or until
underside is well-browned. Turn chicken, cook, covered loosely,
15 more minutes or until browned. (Try to avoid turning chicken
more than 2 times.) Place on absorbent paper to drain. Serve
hot or chilled according to preference or season.

A Confederate standard of excellence. . . .

RIVERMARSH ROAST CHICKEN   Serves 4

4-5 pound **roasting chicken** *or* **capon**, washed
1/2 **lemon**
Salt and **pepper**
1/2 cup **chicken broth**
3/4 cup **dry white wine** *or* **vermouth**

Pull off lumps of fat from inside chicken cavity and retain. Rub
outside of bird with lemon and squeeze a few drops into cavity.
Sprinkle chicken inside and out with salt and pepper. If there is
stuffing,* place in cavity (3/4's full) and truss securely. Drape
chicken fat over breast and secure with toothpicks. Place
chicken on a rack in shallow roasting pan lined with foil. Add
broth and wine. Place on middle shelf of cold oven. Set heat to
350°. Roast 1 3/4 hours if stuffed or 1 1/2 hours if not stuffed.
Baste every 20 minutes with pan juices.

Stuffing:
1/4 pound (1 stick) **butter**
1/4 pound ground **sausage meat**
1/2 cup **chicken broth**
2 teaspoons **poultry seasoning**
2 cups package **stuffing**

Melt butter in skillet. Add sausage and saute 4 minutes. Stir in
broth and poultry seasoning. Add package stuffing and mix well.
Cook covered over medium heat for 5 minutes.

*Adjust roasting time for different weight chickens—allow 26 to
28 minutes per pound. Remember, never undercook a chicken.
Bechemel sauce (page 119) goes well with roast chicken.*

POULTRY

MARYLAND CHICKEN FRICASSEE   Serves 4

4 pound roasting or stewing **chicken**, quartered
1 each: **carrot, celery stalk,** and **onion**, sliced
1/2 teaspoon **cracked pepper**
Water
1 can (10 oz.) **cream of chicken soup**, undiluted
1 cup **light cream**
2 teaspoons fresh **lemon juice**
2 **egg yolks,*** slightly beaten (optional)
1/2 teaspoon **salt**
2 tablespoons **parsley**, chopped
Dash of **mace** (optional)

   *The yolks are more for color than consistency.

Place chicken in stewpot with carrot, celery, onion, pepper, and
enough water to cover. Bring just to a boil. Reduce heat and
simmer 1 3/4 hours or until tender. Remove chicken from
stewpot. When cool enough to handle, remove and discard all
skin, bones, and gristle. Combine soup, cream, lemon juice,
yolks, salt, and parsley. Put chicken pieces in well-buttered
baking dish and add the sauce. Put in cold oven, turn heat to
300° and bake for 40 minutes. Sprinkle with mace before serving.

Note — The liquid left in the stewpot can be strained and kept
for chicken stock.

*A short-cut way for preparing a dish which is very old and very
delicious.*

GRILLED CHICKEN MARINADE   Serves 4-6

2 **broiler-fryer chickens,** * quartered and washed

Marinade:
3 tablespoons fresh **lemon juice**
2 tablespoons **Dijon mustard**
1/4 cup **oil**
2 tablespoons **lemon-pepper marinade**
1 teaspoon **salt**
1/4 cup **dry white wine**

   *Turkey is an excellent alternative. Have your butcher cut turkey into appropriate size pieces. Adjust cooking time to insure meat is properly done.

Combine ingredients for marinade. Mix with chicken and let stand at least 2 hours at room temperature. Grill 35 to 40 minutes or until tender, turning once. (Cooking time will vary according to how hot the fire and its distance from the chicken.) To broil, cook 20 to 25 minutes about 4" from heat source, turning once. Transfer to warmed platter, cover, and let stand 10 minutes before serving.

An easy and delicious respite from grilled beef.

ROAST WILD DUCK   **Serves 2**

2 wild **ducks**, plucked and washed
Vinegar
Salt and **pepper**
2 stalks **celery**, cut into 1" pieces
2 medium **yellow onions**, peeled and quartered
2 **apples**, quartered
2 strips **bacon**

Thoroughly wash ducks. Wipe inside and out with cloth
dampened with vinegar. Lightly salt and pepper birds inside and
out. Stuff cavities with celery, onion and apple (this stuffing
provides moisture and flavor—it is not intended to be eaten).
Cover breasts with bacon and place birds in roasting pan lined
with foil. Place in cold oven and turn heat to 450° and roast as
follows:

> 45 minutes - for large ducks
> 35-40 minutes - for medium-size ducks
> 30-35 minutes - for small ducks

Remove from oven and let stand covered 10 minutes before
carving.

*Moist and tender, and just a little pink. Try with game sauce
and bread sauce (pages 123 & 120).*

ROAST WILD GOOSE   Serves 2

1 wild **goose**, plucked and washed
Salt and **pepper**
3 stalks **celery**, chopped
2 **apples**, quartered
2 medium **yellow onions**, quartered
2 strips **bacon**
3/4 cup **dry sherry** (optional)
1/4 cup **butter**, melted

Lightly salt and pepper the bird inside and out. Stuff cavity with celery, apples, and onions (this stuffing provides moisture and flavor—it is not intended to be eaten). Truss the cavity. Cover breast with bacon strips. Place in roasting pan lined with foil.

Slow method: Roast in 350° oven allowing 22 minutes to the pound or until leg joints can be moved easily. Add sherry after goose begins to brown. Baste frequently with butter and pan juices.

Fast method: Place in cold oven. Turn heat to 450° and roast for 60 minutes. Baste with sherry, butter and pan juices.

Of all wild game, the goose is one of the most difficult to cook properly. When done right, you will experience a flavor that is very special. This bird is even better when served with bread sauce (page 120) and game sauce (page 123).

BREAST OF WILD GOOSE   Serves 4-6

4 **breasts wild goose**
1/2 cup **dry red wine***
1/4 cup **soy sauce**
1/2 cup **vegetable oil**

   *Substitute whiskey for a stronger flavor.

Marinate breasts 3 hours in wine, soy sauce and oil. Grill, pan-
broil or broil the same as an equivalent steak—best when
cooked to medium-rare. Cover and let stand 5 minutes. Carve
breasts diagonally like a London broil.

*Breasting wild geese is very sensible as it is much easier than
cutting and plucking; it leaves the only tender part of the bird;
and it takes little space to store. This superior recipe comes
from the center of goose hunting in the USA—Easton,
Maryland. Serve with lots of game sauce (page 123).*

DEEP SOUTH QUAIL   Serves 4

8 **quail**, dressed and washed

Marinade:
1/4 cup **dry white wine**
1/4 cup **soy sauce**
2 tablespoons **brandy**
1 tablespoon **Worcestershire sauce**
1/2 teaspoon **pepper**
1/4 cup **butter**, melted

Combine all ingredients for marinade except butter in large bowl.
Place quail in marinade and let stand at room temperature for

2 hours. Remove birds from marinade and place them in a shallow baking pan lined with foil. Brush with melted butter and broil for 12 minutes or until browned. Pour marinade with remaining butter over birds and bake at 325° for 20 minutes, basting once. For a sauce, simply degrease pan juices.

A very special Tallahassee recipe for a very special game bird.

ROAST PHEASANT   Serves 4

2 **pheasant**, dressed and washed
1 package (8 oz.) **herb stuffing**
1/2 cup **pecans**, chopped
2 **apples**, peeled, cored and chopped
2 stalks **celery**, chopped
2 tablespoons **parsley**, chopped
1 cup **dry sherry**
6 strips **bacon**
Salt and **pepper**
1/4 cup **butter**, melted

Preheat oven to 425°. Prepare stuffing according to package directions. Add pecans, apples, celery, and parsley and mix thoroughly. Stuff birds 2/3's to 3/4's full and truss. Cover as much as possible of each bird with the bacon strips. Place birds in shallow roasting pan and add sherry. Sprinkle lightly with salt and pepper. Put on middle shelf of oven and reduce heat to 325°. Cook 1 hour and 10 minutes or until tender. Baste every 15 minutes with butter and pan juices.

This recipe solves the normal problem of dry pheasant. End results are moist, succulent, and irresistible.

Fish and Shellfish

Two of the most important and popular food staples in the world are fish and shellfish. Found in virtually every ocean, lake, and river on earth, these foods are readily available either frozen or fresh.

How much to buy:
WHOLE (dressed)
   allow 1 lb. for 1 serving
PAN DRESSED (head, tail and fins removed)
   allow 1 lb. for 2 servings
STEAKS (cross section slices)
   allow 1 lb. for 2 or 3 servings
FILLETS
   allow 1 lb. for 3 or 4 servings
Basic methods of preparation:
   DRY HEAT (bake, broil, barbecue)
   MOIST HEAT (poach, steam)
   PAN-FRY
   DEEP-FRY

TETON TROUT   Serves 2

2 strips **bacon**
2 pan-size (9-11") **trout**, cleaned
1/2 cup **milk**
1/4 cup fine **bread crumbs, corn meal** or **flour**
1/2 teaspoon each **salt** and **pepper**
1 tablespoon **butter**
2 wedges **lemon**

Fry bacon in skillet. Remove bacon to absorbent paper and
save—leave drippings in skillet. Dip fish in milk, let drain and
then lightly dredge with combined bread crumbs, salt, and
pepper. Melt butter in pan drippings. Saute trout 6 minutes on
one side over medium-high heat. Turn and spoon grease over
fish. Cook about 5 more minutes or until well-browned. Serve on
warmed plates with bacon and lemon wedges.

*Fresh trout fried to perfection is an experience long
remembered.*

SEVICHE   Serves 4

1 pound fresh **fish fillets** *and/or* **shellfish,** cut in 1/4″ pieces
Suggested choices used separately or in any combination:
pompano   bass   scallops
flounder   haddock   shrimp
red snapper   whitefish
1/4 cup fresh **lime** *or* **lemon juice**
1 large **tomato,** peeled and diced
1/3 cup **oil**
2 small **chilies,** seeded and diced *or* 1/4 teaspoon **Tabasco sauce**
1/2 teaspoon **oregano**
1 1/2 teaspoons **coriander,** cracked
1/2 teaspoon **salt**
1/4 teaspoon **pepper**

In porcelain bowl or glass jar combine well all ingredients and
refrigerate overnight; if time does not allow, then let stand at
room temperature for 4 hours, stirring gently once or twice.
Refrigerate at least 1 hour before serving.

*This is not a raw fish dish. The acid in the lemon or lime juice
"cooks" the fish and shellfish completely. This specialty is a big
favorite along both coasts of Mexico. It's perfect for a light
summer lunch.*

SANDBAR BAKED FISH   Serves 8

1 whole **fish*** (about 4 lbs.), pan dressed
Suggested choices:
bluefish   stripped bass
cod   red snapper
haddock   pompano
mackerel   whitefish
1 teaspoon **salt**
1 cup **milk**
1/2 cup fine **bread crumbs**
2 tablespoons **butter**

   *If frozen, allow to thaw thoroughly before cooking.

Preheat oven to 450°. Soak fish 3 minutes in salted milk. Drain and roll in bread crumbs. Place in shallow baking pan lined with foil and greased. Dot top of fish with butter. Allow 10 minutes cooking time per inch thickness or until fish flakes easily when pierced with a fork. Serve fish on warmed platter.

Plain, simple and absolutely delicious. Remember, the fresher the fish, the better the dish.

BROILED FISH

Serves 6-8

2 pounds **fish steaks**,* cut 1″ thick
    or
2 pounds **fish fillets***
1/4 cup **butter**, melted
1 ounce **dry white wine** *or* **vermouth**
Salt and **pepper**
Lemon wedges

*If frozen, thaw thoroughly before cooking.

Turn heat to broil. Place fish in broiler pan which has been lined with foil and buttered. Place fish in pan, brush with butter and add wine. Put about 4″ from heat. Allow 8 to 10 minutes broiling time per inch thickness. When half the cooking time has elapsed, baste with pan juices. (It is not necessary to turn fish.) Salt and pepper to taste and serve with lemon wedges.

All very simple with unbeatable results.

LOBSTER POTS   Serves 4

2 ripe **melons**, halved with seeds and fiber removed
Choose any one of the following:
cantaloupe
crenshaw
honeydew
3 tablespoons **mayonnaise**
1 1/4 teaspoon fresh **lemon** or **lime juice**
1/2 teaspoon **horseradish**
1/2 ounce **gin** or **light rum** (optional)
1 pound cooked **lobster meat**,* cut in 1/2" pieces

   *Or crab meat.

Cut out melon balls with scoop or spoon from each melon half;
retain the skins. Combine mayonnaise, lemon juice, horseradish,
and gin, and mix with lobster and melon balls. Fill melon halves
with mixture. Cover and refrigerate at least 1 hour. Serve on
bed of cracked ice.

Perfect for a warm weather meal.

SOFT-SHELL CRABS   Serves 2

4 medium-sized fresh **soft-shell crabs**, cleaned*
1 cup **milk**
1/2 cup **flour**
2 tablespoons each **butter** and **oil**
Lemon wedges

   *Ask at your local fishmarket how to properly clean crabs before cooking.

Dip crabs in milk and dust lightly with flour. In heavy skillet
saute crabs in butter and oil over medium heat for 5 minutes on
each side or until slightly crisp (crabs will "spit" if cooked over
too high a heat). Serve with lemon wedges.

*Few items from the sea can equal this magnificent taste treat
which is harvested from the tidewaters of the mid-Atlantic.*

SOUTH SHORE CRAB CAKES   Serves 4

1 pound **crab meat**,* in lumps
2 slices **white bread**, trimmed and cut into 1/4" pieces
1 **egg**, slightly beaten
2 tablespoons **mayonnaise**
1 tablespoon **Dijon mustard**
2 tablespoons **fresh parsley**, finely chopped
1/4 teaspoon each **salt** and **pepper**
5 **saltines**, finely crumbled
2 tablespoons each **butter** and **oil**

  *Preferably fresh.

Combine bread, egg, mayonnaise, mustard, parsley, salt, and
pepper. Add crab meat and gently toss with fork. Form into 8
crab cakes. Dip into saltine crumbs. Sauté crab cakes in butter
and oil on medium-high heat until light brown—about 2 minutes
on both sides.

*When summer is here and the crab season is on, remember this
recipe.*

SAVORY SCALLOPS   Serves 4

2 pounds fresh **scallops**
Boiling **water**
1/2 teaspoon each **salt** and **pepper**
1/3 cup fine **bread crumbs** *or* **flour**
2 tablespoons each **butter** and **oil**
Lemon wedges

Place scallops in bowl and add enough boiling water to cover.
Let stand 3 minutes. Drain and place on paper towels to dry.
Dredge with combined salt, pepper and bread crumbs. Stir fry or
broil in butter and oil for 5 minutes or until pale brown—do not
overcook. Serve with lemon wedges.

Bay scallops are smaller and reputedly more tender and
flavorful than sea scallops. For certain, bay scallops are the
more expensive of the two, however, if cooked properly the only
noticeable difference will be their size.

STEAMED LOBSTER

1 lobster per person

1 quart **sea water** or **salted water***
4 live **lobsters** (1 1/2 to 2 pounds each)
1/4 pound **butter**, melted
4 **lemon wedges**

*One tablespoon salt per quart of water.

In large kettle bring water to boil. Drop lobsters in head first.
Cover and return water to rolling boil. Cook 7 minutes
(10 minutes for lobsters over 2 pounds). Serve with melted
butter and lemon wedges. For cold lobster, simply chill 1 1/2
hours after cooking and serve with mayonnaise and lemon
wedges.

*Lobster is eaten in many parts of the world, but few if any
lobsters compare with the delicate flavor of a Maine lobster.
Contrary to popular belief, lobsters over 2 pounds are just as
tender and tasty as smaller lobsters if cooked properly. In fact,
larger lobsters are better bargains pound for pound.*

SHRIMP PARADISO   Serves 8

3 cloves **garlic**, finely chopped
1/4 pound (1 stick) **butter**
3 tablespoons **olive oil**
1/2 teaspoon **thyme**
30 (about 2 lbs.) raw large **shrimp**, deveined and butterflied*
1/2 tablespoon **salt**
1/2 teaspoon **pepper**

   *To butterfly shrimp, simply run a knife down the center separating the meat and splitting the shell just to the tail.

In heavy saucepan sauté garlic in butter and oil for 2 minutes over medium heat. Remove from heat and stir in thyme. Thoroughly dunk shrimp in seasoned butter and place— shell up—on cookie sheets. Sprinkle with salt and pepper. Broil 3 to 4" from heat for 5 to 7 minutes or until shells become brown and crisp.

The equivalent weight of medium-sized shrimp can be substituted to make appetizers. In Mexico the crispy shells are eaten together with the meat; the contrast of consistencies adds to the enjoyment of this great dish.

SAILOR'S SHRIMP

Serves 4-6

1 quart **water**
1 bottle (12 oz.) **beer**
1 slice **lemon or lime**
1 **bay leaf**
8 **peppercorns**
1 tablespoon **salt**
30 (about 2 lbs.) raw large **shrimp** with shells

Place all ingredients except shrimp in pot. Bring to boil and add shrimp. Return to boil and cook 4 minutes or until tender. Drain. Serve hot in the shell—easily removed—or discard shell, devein and refrigerate to serve chilled.

It is difficult to equal the exquisite, totally unique taste of fresh shrimp.

Casseroles, Chili, Curries and Stews

Preparing any of these recipes is more of an art than a talent. The reason is simply the many ingredients which comprise these dishes. Varying the amounts of the ingredients can pronouncedly alter the taste of a dish, ie. adding more curry for a stronger, more pungent flavor or more chili powder and red pepper for an added touch of "authenticity." With slight adjustments you will find the combination which best suits your taste.

Two big advantages of these recipes is that they can be made in advance and refrigerated or frozen until ready to use and that leftovers always seem to taste better.

COCK-A-DOODLE-DOO

Serves 4-6

2 **broiler-fryer chickens**, cut into serving pieces,
    washed and dried
1/2 cup **flour**
4 tablespoons **butter**
1/4 cup **oil**
1 teaspoon **salt**
1/2 teaspoon **pepper**
4 **yellow onions**, sliced
2 cloves **garlic**, finely chopped
1/2 pound **mushrooms**, washed and sliced
1/2 teaspoon **thyme**
2 **bay leaves**
1 cup **chicken broth** or **consomme**
1/4 cup **dry white wine**
1/4 cup **brandy**

Dredge chicken pieces in flour. Melt 2 tablespoons butter in oil
in large, heavy skillet. Fry chicken, covered, for 5 minutes on
each side. Transfer to large casserole or baking dish. Sprinkle
with salt and pepper. Add remaining ingredients except brandy
around chicken and dot with remaining butter. Cover loosely
and put in cold oven. Turn heat to 325° and bake 50 minutes.
Uncover, gently mix and bake 20 more minutes. Remove from
heat and add brandy.

*The best chicken recipe north of the Mason-Dixon line. Serve
lots of white rice (page 100).*

TEXAS CHILI   **Serves 8-10**

1/4 cup **bacon fat** *or* **oil**
2 medium **yellow onions**, chopped
2 cloves **garlic**, chopped
4 medium **red peppers**, seeded and chopped
      or
1/2 teaspoon **cayenne**
3 pounds fresh **ground beef**
4 tablespoons **flour**
1 can (8 oz.) **tomato sauce**
1 can (32 oz.) **tomatoes**, crushed
2 cups **beef broth**
1/4 cup **chili powder**
1 teaspoon **oregano**
1 1/2 teaspoons **cumin**
1 1/2 teaspoons **salt**
2 tablespoons **vinegar**
1 can (16 oz.) **kidney** *or* **pinto beans*** (optional)

  *Cover with cold water and soak overnight.

Melt fat in large, heavy pot. Add onions, garlic, and peppers, and
sauté over medium heat for 2 minutes. Add meat and cook until
grayish—about 4 minutes. Stir in flour, then add remaining
ingredients. Cover and bring to boil. Reduce heat and simmer
1 1/2 hours, stirring occasionally. Add beans to chili with
30 minutes left to cook. Skim off any surface fat.

*Aficionados of this dish may not approve, but adding the beans
makes a great fillip. This recipe has championship quality. Vary
chili and red pepper proportions to get the "alarm level" which
best suits your palate.*

SHEPHERD'S PIE

Serves 4-6

Filling:
1 can (10 oz.) **cream of chicken soup**, undiluted
1/2 cup **onion**, finely chopped
1/3 cup **celery**, finely chopped
1/4 teaspoon **marjoram**
1/2 teaspoon **salt**
3 cups cooked **lamb**,* hashed

*Any leftover meat or poultry may be used in this dish with great results.

Potato crust:
2 cups **instant mashed potatoes**
2 tablespoons **butter**
1 **egg**, slightly beaten
1 tablespoon **parsley**, chopped

Grease 2 1/2-quart casserole dish with butter. Prepare mashed potatoes. Combine all ingredients for filling except the lamb in a heavy saucepan and bring to boil. Remove from heat and add lamb and half the mashed potatoes. Put into casserole dish. Stir egg into remaining potatoes and add to casserole spreading evenly over top. Place in cold oven, set heat to 400° and bake 40 minutes or until potato crust browns. Sprinkle with parsley and serve.

Remember this delicious dish when you have some leftover lamb.

MAGIC CASSEROLE   Serves 6-8

1 large **yellow onion**, chopped
1 **green pepper**, seeded and chopped
1 tablespoon each **butter** and **oil**
1 1/2 pounds **ground beef** (round or chuck)
1 package (3 oz.) **cream cheese**
1 container (8 oz.) **cottage cheese**
1 container (8 oz.) **sour cream**
1 package (9 oz.) **frozen chopped spinach**, thawed and drained
  drained
1 can (16 oz.) **tomato sauce**
8 ounces **noodles**, boiled al dente
1 teaspoon **oregano**
3/4 teaspoon each **salt** and **pepper**
4 slices **Mozzarella cheese**, cut into 1/2″ strips
1/4 cup grated **Parmesan cheese**

In a large skillet sauté onion and pepper in butter and oil for
2 minutes. Add meat and cook 7 more minutes, stirring once.
Meanwhile, combine cream cheese, cottage cheese, and sour
cream with spinach. Pour tomato sauce into 3-quart casserole
dish. Then layer with noodles and sprinkle evenly with oregano,
salt, and pepper. Then layer with meat mixture and then spinach
mixture. Top with strips of Mozzarella and sprinkle with
Parmesan cheese. Put in cold oven, set heat to 325° and bake
1 1/4 hours.

*A crowd pleaser from D.C. Serve with aromasia garlic bread (page
132).*

CURRIED CHICKEN   Serves 8

2 medium **yellow onions,** chopped
2 tart **apples,** cored, pared and diced
4 tablespoons **butter**
1 teaspoon **salt**
2 or 3 tablespoons **curry powder*** (mild or hot)
2 cans (10-oz. size) **cream of chicken soup,** undiluted
2 cups **milk****
4 pounds (approx. 8 cups) cooked **chicken,** cut into 1" pieces

   *For a more exotic flavor also add 1 teaspoon each tumeric and cumin.
   **If available, use coconut milk.

In large, heavy skillet or stewpot sauté onions and apples in
butter for 4 minutes, stirring gently. Add salt and curry. Mix in
soup and milk. Cook over low heat for 20 minutes or until
boiling. Add chicken, cover and simmer for 45 minutes, stirring
occasionally. If too thick, add more milk.

*A delicious answer for using up any leftover poultry. Tradi-
tionally served with white rice and with any or all of the
following:*

chutney	*chopped egg white*
mashed bananas	*chopped egg yolk*
chopped peanuts	*raisins*
chopped onion	*shredded coconut*

good

TUNA SAINT JACQUES   Serves 6-8

2 cans (7-oz. size) **tuna fish**, drained
1 cup **sour cream**
1 can (10 oz.) **cream of chicken soup**,* undiluted
2 cups **noodles**, boiled al dente
1 cup **dry white wine**
1/2 teaspoon **salt**
1/4 teaspoon **pepper**
1/2 cup **scallions**, sliced
1 1/4 cups fresh **celery**, chopped
3/4 pound fresh **mushrooms**, washed, stemmed and sliced
3 tablespoons **butter**
1/4 cup grated **Parmesan cheese**
2 tablespoons **parsley**, chopped

*Or cream of mushroom or celery soup.

Combine tuna fish, sour cream, soup, cooked noodles, wine,
salt and pepper. Sauté scallions, celery, and mushrooms in
butter for 4 minutes, then add to tuna mixture and turn into
buttered 2-quart casserole. Sprinkle top with cheese and parsley.
Cover, place in cold oven, turn heat to 350° and bake
50 minutes. Serve with toasted English muffins or toast.

A seafood rarely treated so elegantly.

LAMB STEW   Serves 4-6

2 pounds lean **stewing lamb**,* cut in 1″ pieces
2 tablespoons each **oil** and **butter**
2 cloves **garlic**, sliced
2 tablespoons **flour**
1 teaspoon **salt**
3/4 teaspoon **pepper**
1 cup **dry white wine**
1 can (10 oz.) **chicken broth**
1/2 teaspoon **marjoram**
1 **bay leaf**
Hot **water**
4 **carrots**, scraped and cut in 2″ pieces
8 **white onions**, peeled
4 medium **boiling potatoes**, peeled and quartered

*Or leftover meat from rare roast or butterfly lamb.

Brown meat in oil and butter in large, heavy skillet or Dutch oven. Add garlic, flour, salt, and pepper, and cook 2 minutes. Add wine, broth, marjoram, bay leaf, and, if necessary, enough hot water to cover meat. Cover and slow simmer (or bake at 200°) for 1 1/2 hours or until meat is tender. Stir occasionally. Add carrots, onions, and potatoes, and simmer 30 more minutes.

Try this with aromasia garlic bread (page 132), a delicate salad, and a few bottles of your favorite wine.

BEEF BOURGUIGNON   Serves 4-6

2 pounds lean **beef chuck** or **rump**, cut in 1" pieces
3 tablespoons **oil**
3 large **yellow onions**, coarsely chopped
3 tablespoons **flour**
1/3 teaspoon **thyme**
1 **bay leaf**
1 teaspoon **salt**
1/2 teaspoon **ground pepper**
2-3 cups hot **water**
1 bottle **red burgundy**
1/2 pound fresh **mushrooms**, washed and thick sliced
1/4 cup **brandy**
2 tablespoons **parsley**, chopped

Brown meat in oil over medium-high heat in large pot or Dutch
oven. Reduce heat to medium, add onions and cook 3 minutes.
Remove from heat and mix in flour, thyme, bay leaf, salt and
pepper. Then slowly stir in 2 cups hot water and then the
burgundy; if necessary, add more water to completely cover
meat. Cover and slow simmer (or bake at 200°) for 4 hours.
With 20 minutes left to cook, stir in mushrooms. Remove from
heat and stir in brandy. Sprinkle with parsley and serve.

*A great French classic which is easy to prepare and is perfectly
complemented by a salad, a bottle or two of burgundy, and
aromasia garlic bread (page 132).*

BEEF STEW

Serves 4-6

2 pounds **beef chuck** or **rump**, cut in 1" pieces
2 tablespoons each **oil** and **butter**
4 medium **yellow onions**, peeled and quartered
1 **green pepper**, seeded and sliced
3 tablespoons **flour**
1 can (10 oz.) **beef broth**
1 can (20 oz.) stewed **tomatoes**
2 tablespoons **Worcestershire sauce**
1 1/2 teaspoons **salt**
3/4 teaspoon **ground pepper**
Hot **water**
6 medium **boiling potatoes**, peeled and quartered
4 medium **carrots**, scraped and cut in 2" pieces

Brown meat in oil and butter in large, heavy skillet or Dutch
oven. Add 1 onion and the green pepper and cook 3 minutes.
Stir in flour and cook 3 more minutes. Add broth, stewed
tomatoes, Worcestershire sauce, salt, and pepper and, if
necessary, enough hot water to cover meat. Cover tightly and
slow simmer (or bake at 200°) for 3 hours or until meat is
tender (better grades of meat take less time). Stir occasionally.
Add potatoes, carrots, and remaining onions and simmer 30
more minutes adding more hot water if necessary. Adjust seasoning to taste and serve.

*A little effort to get a classic which should be accompanied by
lots of bread and butter, beer, and salad. Out West this stew is
called slumgullion.*

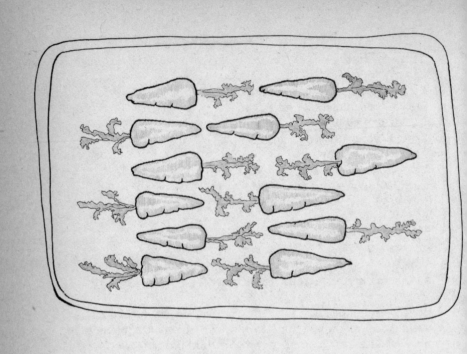

Vegetables, Rice and Potatoes

Vegetables: There are some 40 varieties of vegetables from acorn squash to zucchini which are commercially available in the USA. Because of modern storage methods and year-round growing seasons in California and Florida all but a few vegetables are at your local market any time of the year. Again, it is the simplest of preparations which is the best way to treat vegetables so their full, fresh flavor can be enjoyed. When cooking or seasoning vegetables, always use sea salt, if available.

Rice: Man has been consuming rice before recorded time. Today it is the main food staple of 40% of the world's population. There are four basic varieties of rice; short-grained, long-grained, brown and wild. Hints on cooking rice:

Keep liquid above boiling point.

If needed, add boiling liquid (never cold) to boiling rice.

To stir always use a fork and use a gentle lifting motion.

BAKED ACORN SQUASH   Serves 4

2 fresh **acorn squash**, halved with seeds and fiber removed
8 teaspoons **butter**
4 teaspoons **brown sugar**
Nutmeg
1 cup **water**

Prick interior of each half several times with fork. Put
2 teaspoons butter and 1 teaspoon brown sugar in each half.
Sprinkle each with a dash of nutmeg. Put on rack in shallow
baking pan and add water to the bottom of the pan. Place in
cold oven, set heat at 375° and bake 1 hour or until interior is
fork tender.

*Ease of preparation with delicious results should make you
remember this vegetable more often.*

BUBBLE AND SQUEAK   Serves 4

3 cups leftover **boiled cabbage**
3 cups leftover **mashed potatoes**
1/2 teaspoon **salt**
1/4 teaspoon **ground pepper**
2 tablespoons **butter**
1 tablespoon **oil**

Combine potatoes and cabbage, and season with salt and
pepper. Make 10 or 12 patties and sauté in butter and oil for
about 7 minutes on each side or until lightly browned.

This is a delicious English dish which is used to consume left-overs of their favorite vegetables. For variety, codfish or sausage are added for extra flavor. The derivation of the name Bubble and Squeak is a mystery.

ARTICHOKES   Serves 4

4 fresh **artichokes**, prepared*
4 quarts **salted water**
1 tablespoon **olive oil**
6 **peppercorns**
1 **bay leaf**
2 **lemon peels**

  *Cut stem close to base. Cut off 1/2" of top. Remove small, lower leaves. Snip thorny tip off each leaf with scissors.

Place all ingredients except artichokes in large pot (preferably not iron or aluminum). Bring water to boil. Add artichokes and simmer, uncovered, for 40 to 45 minutes or until a leaf pulls off easily.

A seasonal (September-May) vegetable that is sensational served with either melted butter or hollandaise sauce (page 125).

STRING BEANS   Serves 4

1 1/2 quarts **salted water**
1 pound fresh **string beans**, washed, trimmed and chilled

Bring water to rolling boil. Add beans, return to boil and cook about 15 minutes or until just tender—do not overcook. (Less time is required if beans are french-style—sliced in half.) Drain and transfer to a warmed serving dish. Add the following sauce and serve.

Sauce:
2 cloves **garlic**, sliced
1 tablespoon **butter**
1 tablespoon **oil**
1/2 teaspoon **salt**
1/4 teaspoon **pepper**
1/3 teaspoon **thyme**

Sauté garlic in butter and oil for 2 minutes. Discard garlic pieces. Remove from heat and stir in remaining seasoning.

This recipe is simple yet sophisicated. Getting the vegetable as cold as possible—without freezing—before boiling (or steaming) is the trick to retaining the color and fresh taste of vegetables. This method should be used for preparing asparagus, broccoli, Brussel sprouts, carrots, and peas.

OLD FASHIONED BOSTON
BAKED BEANS
Serves 4-6

1 pound **white Michigan (navy) pea beans**, soaked 12 hours
  in lots of water
1/2 cup **brown sugar**, squeeze out all lumps
1/3 cup **molasses**
1 1/2 teaspoons **dry mustard**
1 medium **yellow onion**, chopped
1/4 teaspoon **pepper**
1/3 pound lean **salt pork**, sliced
      or
1/3 pound lean **bacon**, sliced
Water

Drain and combine beans with brown sugar, molasses, mustard,
onions, and pepper. Transfer to baking dish. Place salt pork over
beans (some may be mixed in with the beans). Add enough
water to cover beans. Prebake, covered tightly, at 325° for
6 hours. Stir once and add more water if necessary. Take out
1/2 cup beans and mash thoroughly with fork. Stir back into
baking dish. Two hours before serving, bake uncovered at 275°.

To make 'em right, you got to bake 'em long.

BUTTERED BEETS   Serves 6-8

2 pounds **fresh beets**, topped and washed
2 quarts **water**
2 tablespoons **butter**
Salt and **pepper** to taste

Boil beets in water over medium-low heat for 1 hour or until
tender. Drain. Hold beets under tap water and slip off skins. If
small, leave whole, otherwise slice, quarter, or dice. Keep hot in
double boiler over simmering water. Just before serving, add
butter and season to taste.

Harvard Beets:
1/2 cup **sugar**
1/2 cup **cider vinegar**
1 tablespoon **cornstarch**
2 whole **cloves**

Put all ingredients in double boiler and heat until clear and
smooth. Add beets from above recipe and heat but do not boil.

*Fresh beets are too often ignored or forgotten as a "second
vegetable." Chilled and sliced, they make a colorful and tasty
addition to summer salads.*

CHAYOTE   Serves 4

2 medium **chayote**
1 quart **water**
3 tablespoons **butter**
1/2 teaspoon **dill** (optional)
Salt and freshly **ground pepper**

Parboil in water for about 15 minutes. When cool enough to
handle, remove skin with potato peeler. Then cut in half
lengthwise. Remove and discard pit. Cut vegetable into 1/2"
cubes or 1/4" slices. Steam or boil in lightly salted water until
fork tender—do not overcook. Drain, add butter and season to
taste.

*This very delicious representative of the squash family is avidly
consumed in Mexico, Central and South America, North Africa,
Bermuda, and the Caribbean. It is known by other names such
as Christophine, Chocho, xuxu, Vegetable Pear, pepinella,
Custard Marrow, brionne and mirliton. In the past few years
this superb vegetable has become increasingly available in
markets throughout the USA.*

CORN ON THE COB   Serves 4

3 quarts **water** (with 2 tablespoons salt)
8 ears **fresh corn**, husked
1/4 pound (1 stick) **butter**
Salt and **pepper**

Bring salted water to boil in large kettle. Add corn and boil,
uncovered, for 6 to 8 minutes or until just fork tender. Popularly
served with butter, salt and pepper. To keep corn hot until
ready to serve, cover pot and leave corn in the water with the
heat off.

*A warm summer's meal is hardly complete without an offering
of fresh corn. Sweet, white corn is the most desirable variety
and takes only about 4 minutes to cook.*

MASTERFUL MUSHROOMS
Serves 4

1 pound **fresh mushrooms**, washed, stemmed and quartered
1 tablespoon **butter**
1/3 teaspoon **thyme**
Salt and **ground pepper** to taste

Melt butter in double boiler. Add mushrooms and thyme, and gently stir. Cover and cook over simmering water for 10 to 15 minutes or until mushrooms begin to give off juice—do not overcook. Season with salt and pepper to taste and serve.

This method of cooking mushrooms maintains their unique fresh flavor. As a second vegetable or combined with other vegetables, the mushroom is extraordinary.

COUNTRY ONIONS   Serves 4

16-18 (1 lb.) **white onions**, peeled
3/4 cup **water**
3 tablespoons **butter**
2 tablespoons **flour**
1/4 teaspoon each **salt** and **white pepper**
1 tablespoon **parsley**, chopped
1/2 cup **chicken broth**
1/2 cup **light cream**

Place onions in saucepan with water. Cover and steam for
20 minutes or until just tender. Meanwhile, in a separate saucepan, melt butter. Stir in flour, salt, pepper, and parsley, and
cook over medium heat for 3 minutes. Remove from heat and
slowly stir in broth and cream. Return to heat and stir until
smooth. Add onions and any water left in saucepan to sauce.
Gently mix with wooden spoon.

*Rarely thought of as a vegetable to be served by itself, onions
are simple to prepare and have a unique taste of their own.*

FRIED ONIONS   Serves 4

1 1/4 pounds **yellow onions,** sliced
3 tablespoons **butter**
1 tablespoon **vegetable oil**
1/2 cup **beef stock** or **broth**
1/2 teaspoon **salt**
1/4 teaspoon **pepper**

Gently saute onions with butter and oil in skillet for 4 minutes.
Add broth, salt, and pepper, and simmer over low heat for 12
minutes.

*If you're looking for a perfect match for hamburger, liver, steaks
or just about any meat, this is the one that everybody forgets
but shouldn't.*

CRISPY-SKIN BAKED POTATOES Serves 4

Over 32 billion pounds of potatoes are produced in the United States every year.

4 medium **baking potatoes**, washed

Preheat oven to 475°. Poke each potato with fork 3 or 4 times lengthwise along a single line—this allows excess moisture to escape. Place in oven and bake 55 minutes. When done, make a cut along fork holes and squeeze ends to open. Season with sour cream and chopped chives, or butter, salt, and pepper.

Note — To get a baked potato with a soft skin, rub with oil, wrap in foil, and bake at 425° for 50 to 55 minutes.

Placing a metal skewer or nail lengthwise through the center of a potato will reduce cooking time to about 35 minutes—however, the skin will not be crunchy.

MASHED POTATOES   Serves 4

4 large **baking potatoes,** * peeled and quartered
2 quarts **water** (with 2 tablespoons salt)
4 tablespoons **butter**
1 cup **milk**
Salt and **pepper** to taste
1 tablespoon **parsley**, chopped

*Do not use boiling potatoes.

Put potatoes in salted water and boil until fork tender—about
20 minutes. Meanwhile, melt butter in milk—do not boil. Mash
potatoes with a fork, or put through a sieve or ricer. Slowly stir
in hot milk mixture and beat until smooth and fluffy. (More liquid
may be added to get desired consistency.) Season to taste.
Sprinkle with parsley and serve.

*Making them fresh is easy and certainly tastes a lot better than
instant.*

WESTERN HASH BROWN POTATOES   Serves 4

4 medium **baking potatoes**, peeled and washed
1 small **onion**, diced
1 teaspoon **salt**
1/4 teaspoon **ground pepper**
2 tablespoons **bacon fat** *or* **oil**
2 tablespoons **butter**

Shred potatoes and spread on absorbent paper to remove some moisture. (Do not let potatoes stand too long before frying as they will discolor.) Place in bowl and combine with onion, salt, and pepper. Heat fat and butter in heavy skillet. Add potatoes and fry over medium-low heat about 25 minutes or until golden brown, turning once.

The real thing. . . .

BOILED FRESH SPINACH   Serves 4

1/4 cup **water**
1 tablespoon **olive oil**
1/4 teaspoon **salt**
1 pound fresh **spinach**, washed and stemmed*

   *Two pounds spinach leaves with stems yields one pound spinach leaves
without stems.

Put water, olive oil, and salt in large pot and bring to boil. Add
spinach and cover. Cook for 4 to 5 minutes stirring once or until
spinach is completely wilted and hot. Quickly drain and serve.

Creamed spinach: Cook spinach as above and drain completely.
Chop in food processor or blender for 5 to 10 seconds. Transfer
to double boiler. Stir in 1/4 cup heavy or sour cream and heat to
serving temperature.

Very fast and very good. . . .

BAKED SWEET POTATOES   Serves 4

4 medium **sweet potatoes**, washed and dried
4 teaspoons **butter**
4 large **marshmallows** (optional)
Ground **nutmeg**

Preheat oven to 475°. With a fork poke each sweet potato 3 or 4 times lengthwise along a single line—this lets excess moisture escape. Bake 45 minutes. When done, cut each sweet potato lengthwise and squeeze ends to open. Place 1 teaspoon butter and 1 marshmallow in each sweet potato. Sprinkle lightly with nutmeg, and serve.

For all intents and purposes, yams and sweet potatoes are the same. The reputed difference is that yams are normally brighter orange and sweeter. Whatever the difference, both are delicious.

BAKED ZUCCHINI

Serves 6-8

Zucchini and squash are fruits, not vegetables.

2 pounds fresh **zucchini**, washed and cut in 1/2" slices
2 quarts **water** (with 2 tablespoons salt)
1 clove **garlic**, minced
2 tablespoons **butter**
1 1/2 cups **sour cream**
1/2 cup **light cream**
1/2 teaspoon **dill**
1/2 cup **bread crumbs**

Boil zucchini in salted water for 5 minutes. Drain and set aside covered. Sauté garlic in butter for 2 minutes and combine with sour cream, light cream and dill. Place zucchini in buttered 2-quart casserole. Pour cream sauce over top and cover with bread crumbs. Place on top rack of cold oven. Set heat to 350° and bake 30 minutes.

Yellow squash or eggplant may be used to substitute for or in any combination with zucchini in preparing this dish.

PERFECT RICE   Serves 4

1 cup **short-grain** *or* **long-grain rice**
2 cups cold **water**
1 tablespoon **butter**
Salt and **pepper** to taste

In saucepan put rice in water and bring to boil, uncovered.
Reduce heat and simmer, covered, for about 14 minutes (20
minutes for long-grain rice) or until rice is tender and water is
absorbed. To keep rice hot until ready to serve, put in a large
sieve and place over steaming water, loosely covered. Add
butter and seasoning just before serving.

*When rice is good, you will know it. And nothing could be
simpler. Most orientals believe that short-grain rice has more
flavor than long-grain. Try cooking rice in chicken or beef broth
instead of water.*

WILD RICE   Serves 4

1 cup **wild rice**
1 1/2 cups **water**
2 tablespoons **butter**,* melted
1 tablespoon **vegetable oil**
Salt

  *Or melted **chicken** or **duck fat**, if available.

Very thoroughly rinse rice in cold water and drain. Put rice and
1 1/2 cups water in double boiler and bring to boil over direct
heat. Reduce to slow simmer and cook, covered, for 30 minutes,
stirring once. Place over simmering water, covered, for 15 minutes or until tender. Before serving, add butter, oil and salt to
taste.

Goes well with all game or poultry meals.

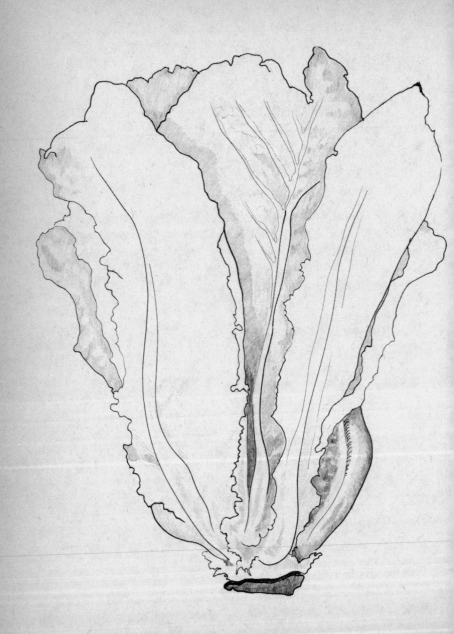

Salads and Dressings

Salads and the dressings that go with them are a cinch to make and a joy to eat, plus their variety is almost limitless. Testing combinations of greens, fruits, and vegetables with different vinegars, oils, and seasoning can be very gratifying—especially when you discover a blend that is uniquely delicious. A salad dressing should always be added just prior to being served, never ahead of time. And remember, "roughage" is good for the digestion, so have it often.

Greens and colorful, tasty extras to choose from:

Greens

arugala
bibb lettuce
Boston lettuce
chicory
endive
escarole
red leaf or
  ruby lettuce

iceberg lettuce
romaine
sorrel
spinach leaf
Swiss chard
watercress

Extras

avocado
beans
bell pepper
broccoli
cabbage
(green and red)
cauliflower
celery
cucumber

hard-boiled eggs
fruit
mushrooms
olives
onions
radishes
sprouts
tomatoes

TOMATO ASPIC

Serves 4-6

1 quart **V-8** *or* **tomato juice**
2 packages **unflavored gelatin**
1 tablespoon fresh **lemon juice**
1 **scallion**, finely chopped

Garnish:
1 small **cucumber**, peeled and sliced
2 hard boiled **eggs**, sliced
Salad greens

Bring 2 cups juice to boil. Remove from heat. Add gelatin and stir until dissolved. Then add remaining 2 cups V-8 juice, lemon juice and chopped scallion. Pour into mold and refrigerate until set—about 2 hours. Unmold* onto chilled platter and garnish.

*To unmold, invert mold onto platter and drape with damp, hot towel for 15 seconds.

An easy recipe that is perfect for a summer lunch or supper.

CAESAR SALAD   **Serves 4**

2 cloves **garlic**, halved
1/2 cup **olive oil**
1/4 cup fresh **lemon juice**
3/4 teaspoon **Dijon mustard**
8-10 **anchovies**, finely shredded
1/2 teaspoon each **salt** and **pepper**
2 heads fresh **romaine lettuce**, washed, dried and chilled
1 raw **egg** (optional)
1/2 cup freshly grated **Parmesan cheese**
2 cups **croutons**

Rub salad bowl with garlic and add oil; let oil absorb garlic flavor
for 30 minutes. Discard any garlic pieces. Add lemon juice,
mustard, anchovies, salt and pepper. Just before serving, break
the lettuce leaves into large pieces and put in salad bowl. Add
the egg and cheese, and toss well. Add the croutons and toss.
Serve immediately.

This magnificent salad can be served as part of a meal or as a
meal by itself.

CELERY RÉMOULADE   Serves 4

1 medium **celery root**, washed, pared and shredded
4 **lettuce** leaves, washed

Rémoulade:
3 tablespoons **mayonnaise**
2 tablespoons **sour cream**
2 teaspoons **oil**
1 teaspoon **Dijon mustard**
1 teaspoon **chervil** (optional)

Combine all ingredients for rémoulade. Place shredded celery root and rémoulade in bowl and toss thoroughly. Chill at least 1 hour. Serve on lettuce leaves.

When in season, this specialty is found as an appetizer on the menus of many great restaurants. It is delicious as either an appetizer or a salad.

FRESH CELERY SALAD   Serves 4

2 bunches fresh **celery**,* washed and chopped
2 tablespoons fresh **lemon**
2 tablespoons cold **water**
1 tablespoon **salad oil** (*not* olive oil)
1 tablespoon fresh **parsley**, finely chopped

  *With leaves, if not wilted.

Place all ingredients in salad bowl. Toss and serve.

Very simple and very tasty.

Excellent

EASTERN SHORE COLESLAW   Serves 6-8

1 3/4 cups **mayonnaise**
1 1/2 tablespoons fresh **lemon juice**
1 teaspoon **sugar**
2 tablespoons **olive oil**
1 teaspoon **salt**
3/4 teaspoon fresh milled **pepper**
1 small **white onion**, finely chopped (optional)
1 medium head raw **green cabbage**,* finely shredded

*Remove and discard outer leaves; pare away core before slicing.

Combine all ingredients, except cabbage, in medium bowl and mix well. When ready to serve, add cabbage and toss until well coated.

Alternatives: Any of the following can be added to the above recipe for different taste preference:

1 tablespoon **caraway seeds**
1 **apple**, peeled, cored, and chopped
2 tablespoons **walnuts**, crushed
1/4 cup **sour cream**

An old standard that can be an extraordinary treat if served fresh. It could not be any easier to prepare.

CHILLED CUCUMBER MOUSSE

Serves 6-8

1 box (3 oz.) **lemon Jello**
1 cup boiling **water**
1 large **cucumber**, pared and diced
1 cup **mayonnaise**
2 cups (1 lb.) **creamed cottage cheese**
1/2 cup **celery**, diced
1 tablespoon **onion**, minced
1 tablespoon **tarragon** *or* **wine vinegar**
1/2 cup **blanched almonds**, chopped
Salad greens

Chill 1 1/2-quart mold. Dissolve Jello in boiling water and cool slightly. Stir in all remaining ingredients except greens. Pour into mold and refrigerate. Allow at least 1 hour to set. Turn out on serving platter. Cover and chill until ready to serve. Garnish with salad greens.

Delicious as a light, summer meal or as a salad.

CURRIED EGG MOUSSE

Serves 6-8

2 cups **chicken broth**
1 tablespoon **curry powder**
2 packages **gelatin**
1/4 cup cold **water**
1 1/2 cups **mayonnaise**
3 hard-boiled **eggs**, grated through strainer
1/3 teaspoon each **salt** and **pepper**
Salad greens

Chill 1 1/2-quart ring-mold. Put broth and curry in saucepan and bring to boil. Dissolve gelatin in water and add to broth. Chill until it begins to thicken—about 20 minutes. Thoroughly stir in mayonnaise, eggs, salt and pepper. Pour into mold and refrigerate until set—about 1 1/2 hours. When ready to serve, turn out onto chilled platter. Line center with salad greens and fill with whatever suits your fancy—try cold shrimp or chicken.

This recipe doubles as either a summer meal or as a light salad course.

LORENZO SALAD

Serves 4-6

1 medium head **green cabbage**, discard limp or damaged
    outer leaves, cut out and discard core, shred, and chill
1 bunch fresh **watercress**, chopped

Dressing:
6 tablespoons **salad oil**
2 tablespoons **red wine vinegar**
1/4 teaspoon **dry mustard**
1/2 teaspoon each **salt** and **pepper**
3 tablespoons **chili sauce** *or* **catsup**

Put all ingredients for dressing in screw-top jar and shake well.
When ready to serve, put cabbage, watercress and dressing in a
salad bowl and toss well.

A perfect blend of texture and flavor.

PALMER'S POTATO SALAD

Serves 4-6

4 medium **boiling potatoes**, washed

Dressing:
1/4 cup **salad oil**
1/2 cup **mayonnaise**
2 tablespoons **dry white wine** (optional)
1/4 cup chopped **onion**
2 hard-boiled **eggs**, grated through strainer
3/4 teaspoon **Dijon mustard**
1 teaspoon **salt**
1/8 teaspoon **white pepper**

Combine all ingredients for dressing. Parboil potatoes in salted water for 30 minutes or until fork tender. Drain and pare while still warm. Slice or cut as desired and mix with dressing. Chill at least 2 hours.

This recipe can also be served hot.

SPINACH SALAD   Serves 4

1 1/2 pounds fresh **spinach**, washed, dried, stemmed and chilled
4 **scallions**, chopped
1/4 pound **mushrooms**, washed and thickly sliced
6 pieces **bacon**, fried crisp and crumbled
1 **egg**, slightly beaten (optional)

Dressing:
1/2 cup **olive oil**
2 tablespoons **lemon juice** *or* **white vinegar**
2 tablespoons **brown sugar**
2 tablespoons **water**
1/2 teaspoon **dry mustard**
1/2 teaspoon each **salt** and **pepper**

bland dressing

Place all ingredients for dressing in screw-top jar and shake well.
Just before serving, break spinach leaves into large bite-size
pieces and place in salad bowl. Add remaining ingredients and
toss with dressing.

A very popular salad done with ease.

TUNA FISH SALAD   Serves 4

2 cans (7-oz. size) **chunk-style tuna fish,** drained
2 stalks **celery**, chopped
4 tablespoons **mayonnaise**
2 tablespoons **sour cream**
1/4 cup **onion**, finely chopped
1 1/2 tablespoons **lemon-pepper marinade**
Salad greens

Combine all ingredients with 2 forks. Serve garnished with salad greens or use for making tuna sandwiches.

HOUSE DRESSING   Yields about 1 cup

3/4 cup **salad** *or* **olive oil**
1/4 cup **vinegar**
2 teaspoons **Dijon mustard**
1/2 teaspoon **Worcestershire sauce**
1/4 teaspoon each **salt** and **ground pepper**

Put all ingredients in screw-top jar and shake well.

Good on any salad. For a final touch after adding dressing to a salad, sprinkle with freshly ground pepper and grated Parmesan cheese.

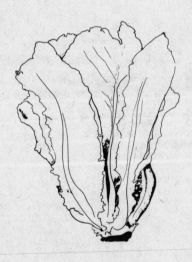

VINAIGRETTE

Yields about 1 cup

1/4 cup **red wine vinegar** or **tarragon vinegar**
1 teaspoon **Dijon mustard**
1 1/2 teaspoons **chives**, finely chopped
1 teaspoon **scallions or shallots**, minced
3/4 teaspoon coarsely **ground pepper**
1/2 teaspoon **salt**
3/4 cup **olive oil**

Place all ingredients in screw-top jar and shake. Refrigerate until ready to serve. Shake well before using.

Additions often made to above recipe:

1 1/2 tablespoons **India relish**
1 hard-boiled **egg**, chopped

Excellent with cold vegetables such as artichoke, string beans and asparagus.

Sauces

A sauce should never be more than a compatible friend to a great personality. When preparing sauces, it will be helpful to remember that the quantity of a sauce added to a dish is as important as the ingredients in that sauce. It is fine to make a sauce which is outstanding on its own, but use too much of that sauce and it could overpower a dish rather than complement it. Ultimately, a sauce should be a perfect blending of tastes in order to set off and intensify the basic ingredient of a dish to which it is added—not unlike the relationship of a picture and its frame.

It should be noted that strong sauces such as curries were often used to disguise the deteriorated state of staple foods. Today, however, with the general availability of fresh foods and refrigeration, such strong seasonings find their strength in subtle rather than overbearing sauces.

Basic Ingredients:

Roux: fat — butter
    lard
    pan drippings

Liquids: beef broth or stock
    chicken broth or stock
    fish stock or clam broth
    veal stock

thickeners — arrowroot
    cornstarch
    egg yolks
    flour

Basic French Sauces:
 Béchamel
 Brown sauce
 Velouté

WESTERN BAR B-QUE SAUCE   Yields about 3 cups

1 1/4 cups **catsup**
1/2 cup **vinegar**
1/4 cup **Worcestershire sauce**
2 medium **yellow onions**, chopped
2 tablespoons **prepared mustard**
1/2 cup **water**
2 tablespoons **sugar**
3 tablespoons **butter**
1 teaspoon **chili powder**
3/4 teaspoon **cayenne**
1/2 **lemon**, juice and rind

Combine all ingredients and simmer, covered, for 30 minutes.

A champion sauce to barbecue anything or as a side dish at any barbecue.

BÉCHAMEL

Yields about 2 cups

1/2 cup **chicken broth**
1/4 cup **dry white wine**
1 small **onion**, sliced
1 **scallion**, sliced
1/2 stalk **celery**, sliced
1 **bay leaf**
Dash of **nutmeg**
1/4 teaspoon each **salt** and **pepper**
4 tablespoons **butter**
4 tablespoons **flour**
3/4 cup **milk**
1/2 teaspoon **tarragon**
2 teaspoons **parsley**

In a saucepan combine broth, wine, onion, scallion, celery, bay leaf, nutmeg, salt and pepper, and simmer covered 10 minutes. Meanwhile, in a separate saucepan, melt butter. Remove from heat and stir in flour. Return to low heat and cook about 3 minutes. Remove from heat and slowly strain broth into roux, stirring constantly. Stir in milk, tarragon and parsley. Keep hot in double boiler over simmering water.

Serve with poultry, veal or vegetables.

BREAD SAUCE

Makes about 3 cups

1 half of **large onion**, peeled
4 **cloves**
1 pint **Half & Half**
2 tablespoons **butter**
2 cups **white bread**

Push cloves into cut portion of onion. Put Half & Half and onion in double boiler. Slowly bring to simmer over direct heat—do not boil. Discard onion and add butter. When butter has melted, add bread and mix thoroughly. Cover and heat over simmering water. To thicken, add more bread or to thin, add more Half & Half; consistency should be thick yet smooth.

*This sauce with either currant jelly or game sauce
(page 123) is the ultimate answer for your favorite game
dishes.*

BROWN SAUCE   Yields about 1 1/2 cups

3 tablespoons **butter**
2 tablespoons **scallions** *or* **shallots**, minced
3 tablespoons **flour**
1 cup **beef broth**, boiling
1 tablespoon **catsup**
1 **bay leaf**
1/4 teaspoon each **thyme** and **tarragon**
1 tablespoon **parsley**, chopped
1/4 cup **dry red wine**

Melt butter in skillet. Sauté scallions for 2 minutes over medium heat. Remove from heat and stir in flour. Return to heat and cook, stirring constantly, until roux begins to brown. Stir in boiling broth. Reduce heat to low. Add remaining ingredients and simmer, covered, 20 minutes, stirring occasionally.

A perfect sauce for your red meat favorites.

FLORADORA SAUCE   Yields about 2 1/2 cups

2 **egg whites**
1/2 cup **confectioners' sugar**
2 **egg yolks**
1 1/2 cups **heavy cream**
1 teaspoon **vanilla extract**
1/2 teaspoon **salt**

Beat egg whites until just stiff, slowly adding 1/4 cup sugar. Then beat egg yolks until thick, gradually adding the remaining sugar. Combine well egg whites and yolks with remaining ingredients.

A fabulous sauce for cakes, ginger bread, and dessert souffles.

GAME SAUCE   Yields about 1 1/2 cups

1 jar (12 oz.) **red currant jelly**
2 tablespoons **Dijon mustard**
3/4 teaspoon **Worcestershire sauce**
1/2 tablespoon **wine vinegar**
1/2 teaspoon **soy sauce**
1/4 teaspoon **ground cumin**
1/8 teaspoon **pepper**

Place all ingredients in saucepan and heat over low flame until jelly has melted. Stir to blend thoroughly. Serve hot.

This sauce is superb with all wild game and even better when served in combination with bread sauce (page 120).

HARD SAUCE   **Yields about 1 1/4 cups**

1 cup **confectioners' sugar**
1/4 cup **butter**, softened
1 tablespoon **rum** *or* **brandy**
1/2 tablespoon boiling **water**
1/2 teaspoon **vanilla extract**
1/8 teaspoon **salt**

In small mixing bowl combine all ingredients. Beat vigorously until well blended. Chill until ready to serve.

An absolutely illegal but scrumptious sauce for warm desserts like apple brown betty (page 138).

HOLLANDAISE   Yields about 1 cup

4 **egg yolks**
2 teaspoons warm **water**
4 teaspoons fresh **lemon juice**
1/4 pound (1 stick) **butter**, melted
1/2 teaspoon **salt**
1/8 teaspoon **white pepper** or **cayenne**

Combine egg yolks, water, and lemon juice in a heavy saucepan. Whisk until frothy—about 2 minutes. Place over low heat, whisking constantly, until sauce reaches smooth, thick consistency. Remove from heat. Slowly add melted butter, beating constantly. Add salt and pepper.

To keep warm: Place in double boiler over simmering water.

To thin: Stir in water 1 tablespoon at a time.

To correct curdling: Add 2 tablespoons cold water and beat vigorously.

The perfect complement to asparagus, broccoli, artichokes and, of course, eggs benedict.

HORSERADISH SAUCE

Yields about 2 cups

1 1/2 cups **sour cream**
4 tablespoons **horseradish**
1/2 cup **beef broth** or **stock**
1/3 teaspoon **salt**
1/4 teaspoon **pepper**

Combine all ingredients in double boiler and heat over simmering water. Serve hot or cold.

A favorite sauce for either boiled or roast beef (pages 33 and 32 respectively).

FRESH MINT SAUCE   **Yields about 1 cup**

1/4 cup **water**
1 1/2 tablespoons **sugar**
2/3 cup **plain** or **tarragon vinegar**
1/4 cup fresh **mint leaves**, finely chopped

Bring water to simmer in small saucepan. Add sugar and stir
until dissolved. Remove from heat and add vinegar and mint.
Before serving, let stand 2 hours at room temperature or
overnight under refrigeration. Serve in sauce bowl at room
temperature or slightly heated.

*This superb sauce is the perfect match for most hot lamb
recipes; curried lamb would be an exception.*

SPICY STEAK SAUCE   **Yields about 1 cup**

3/4 cup **catsup**
2 tablespoons **prepared mustard**
1 tablespoon **vinegar**
3/4 teaspoon **ground pepper**
1/8 teaspoon **Tabasco sauce**

Put all ingredients in double boiler and heat over simmering
water for 10 minutes.

A little bit of this sauce will add some zip to your favorite steak.

SPAGHETTI SAUCE #181   Yields about 4 cups

4 tablespoons **olive oil**
3 cloves **garlic**
2 cans (16-oz. size) **stewed tomatoes**
   or
2 pounds **fresh tomatoes**, peeled* and chopped
3 ounces **tomato paste**
2 medium **yellow onions**, peeled and quartered
1 teaspoon **oregano**
1 teaspoon **salt**
1/2 teaspoon **ground pepper**
2 teaspoons **sweet basil leaves****
3 tablespoons **butter**

   *To facilitate peeling, first submerge tomatoes in boiling water for 20 seconds.
   **Use fresh basil if available.

Put oil in large, heavy saucepan and sauté garlic for
1 minute—do not brown. Stir in remaining ingredients except
basil and butter. Cover and simmer 40 minutes, stirring twice.
With 5 minutes left to cook, remove garlic cloves and stir in basil
and butter. (If using fresh tomatoes, strain through ricer or sieve
to remove seeds.) Serve with freshly boiled pasta.

A tomato sauce supreme...

VELOUTÉ   **Yields about 1 1/2 cups**

3 tablespoons **butter**
3 tablespoons **flour**
2 tablespoons **yellow onion**, chopped
1 cup **chicken** *or* **clam broth**, boiling
1/4 cup **dry white wine**
1/4 teaspoon **thyme**
3/4 teaspoon **salt**
1/2 teaspoon **pepper**
Dash of **paprika**

Melt butter in heavy saucepan. Remove from heat and stir in
flour. Return to low heat and cook about 2 minutes—do not
brown. Add remaining ingredients, cover and slow simmer
20 minutes. Strain and serve.

The *sauce to serve with fish.*

Breads

Baking bread is a creative art by virtue of the many elements involved in its doing. Many people do not bake bread simply because a wide variety of delicious, fresh breads from French baguettes to pumpernickel are available at local markets and bakeries. The following recipes either do not lend themselves to commercial representation—such as popovers—or are elaborations of a readily available bread—for example Aromasia Garlic Bread.

AROMASIA GARLIC BREAD   For 1 loaf

2 cloves **garlic**, finely chopped
1 tablespoon **oil**
1/4 pound (1 stick) **butter**
1 1/2 tablespoons fresh **parsley**, finely chopped
1 teaspoon **dill seed**, crushed
1 loaf **French** or **Italian bread**, sliced diagonally*

   *Only cut 7/8's through the loaf so the pieces will stay together.

Sauté garlic in butter and oil for 3 minutes. Remove from heat
and immediately stir in remaining ingredients. Put loaf in heavy
foil. Spoon garlic butter between each slice. Sprinkle bread
lightly with salt. Close foil. Heat at 300° for 30 minutes.
Serve hot.

Superb with meats, pastas, and stews.

CROUTONS   Makes 1 cup

2 cloves **garlic**, sliced
2 tablespoons **butter**
2 slices **white bread**, trimmed and cut in 1/4" cubes

Sauté garlic in butter for 2 minutes. Discard the garlic.
Reduce heat to low. Add the bread cubes and gently turn to
soak up butter. Cook turning the cubes until evenly crisp and
golden brown. Place on absorbent paper and allow to cool
before using—about 10 minutes.

Perfect with salads and cold creamed soups.

GRIT BREAD

Serves 4

1/2 cup regular **grits**
2 cups **milk**
1/2 teaspoon **salt**
1 **egg**, beaten
1 tablespoon **butter**

Preheat oven to 400°. Grease well a small baking pan or dish. In saucepan heat milk to boiling point and stir in grits and salt. Place over medium-low heat and cook stirring until thick—about 2 minutes. Remove from heat and stir in butter and egg. Pour into baking dish spreading batter to 1/2" thickness. Bake 30 minutes or until top is browned. (The batter will not rise.)

This bread goes extremely well with game and poultry dishes.

PUFFY POPOVERS

Makes 6 popovers

1 cup **flour**
2 **eggs**, slightly beaten
1 cup **milk**
2 tablespoons **butter**, melted
1/2 teaspoon **salt**
Crisco *or* **vegetable oil**

Combine all ingredients except Crisco and beat vigorously or mix in blender for 3 minutes. Let batter rest 15 minutes before baking. Grease well six muffin cups with Crisco. Fill each cup 1/2 to 2/3 full with batter. To bake:

With no preheating—place muffin pan in cold oven. Turn heat to 450° and bake 40 to 45 minutes or until puffed and golden brown.

With preheating—preheat oven to 425°. Bake 30 minutes or until puffed and golden brown.

Note—Avoid opening oven door while popovers are baking.

The ultimate touch for a meal of your favorite beef.

YORKSHIRE PUDDING

Makes 1 pie

1 cup **flour**
2 **eggs**, slightly beaten
1 cup **milk**
2 tablespoons **butter**, melted
1/2 teaspoon **salt**
2 tablespoons **Crisco***

*Use beef or bacon fat if available.

Combine flour, eggs, milk, butter, and salt and beat vigorously.
for 4 minutes. Let batter rest 15 minutes. Grease 10″ pie plate
with Crisco. Pour batter into pie plate, place in cold oven, turn
to 450° for 25 minutes, then lower to 350° and bake
15 minutes or until golden brown.

A delicious tradition with Roast Beef (page 32).

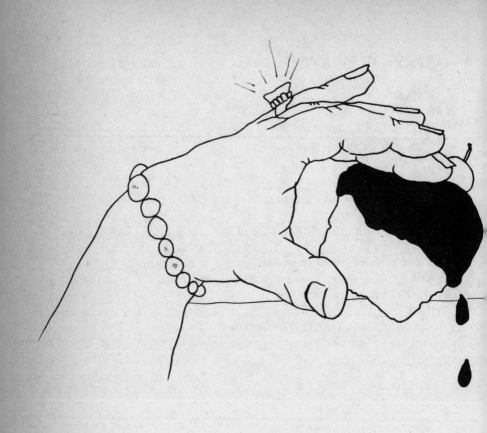

Desserts

Desserts are everyone's favorite. If good, they can make an entire meal rise to stardom.

CRUNCHY APPLE BROWN BETTY   Serves 4-6

1/4 pound (1 stick) **butter**, softened
1 cup **bread crumbs**
4 cups tart cooking **apples**,* peeled, cored, and thin sliced
1 tablespoon fresh **lemon juice**
1 teaspoon **cinnamon**
1 cup **light brown sugar**
1/4 cup **flour**

   *Seven or eight greening or McIntosh apples.

Spread 2 tablespoons of the butter on inside of baking dish.
Sprinkle bottom with 1/4 cup of the bread crumbs. Add sliced
apples and lemon juice, and sprinkle cinnamon and 1/4 cup
sugar over top. Combine remaining butter, bread crumbs and
sugar with the flour and mix until crumbly. Spread evenly over
apples. Put in cold oven, set heat at 350° and bake for
1 1/4 hours or until golden brown on top.

*A super dessert which is always a satisfying surprise for
everyone—especially those who "haven't had it for years." The
final touch is hard sauce (page 124) or vanilla ice cream.*

PALMER ORCHARD APPLESAUCE

**Yields about
1 1/2 quarts**

4 pounds **cooking apples**, washed, cored, and quartered
1 cup **water**
1 cup **light brown sugar**
1/2 teaspoon **cinnamon**

Place prepared apples in large pot or saucepan and add water.
Bring to simmer and cook, covered, until apples are tender—
about 20 minutes. Add more water if needed—older apples
require more water than new apples. Put through strainer and
return strained pulp to pot. Stir in sugar and cinnamon until well
combined. Serve hot or cold.

Add any of the following to the above recipe to suit personal
taste:

2 cups pureed **raspberries**
2 teaspoons fresh **lemon juice**
1/4 teaspoon **nutmeg**

*Homemade applesauce makes a simple but satisfying dessert.
Also it is the traditional item served with just about all pork
dishes.*

BAKED APPLES

Serves 4

4 **baking apples,*** washed and cored (do not peel)
4 tablespoons **honey**
4 tablespoons **sugar**
2 tablespoons **lemon juice**
1 teaspoon **cinnamon** *or* **allspice**

*Rome Beauties and York Imperial are excellent for baking.

Put apples in small, shallow baking pan with 1/2 cup water. Put 1 tablespoon honey in center of each apple. Sprinkle equally with sugar, lemon juice and cinnamon. Place in oven, turn heat to 350° and bake 40 minutes or until tender. Serve hot or chilled.

For a gourmet touch, try this recipe with hard sauce (page 124) or with heavy cream.

BAKED BANANAS

Serves 4

3 tablespoons **butter**
1/4 cup **light brown sugar**
3/4 teaspoon **powdered ginger**
1/3 cup fresh **orange juice**
2 teaspoons fresh **lemon juice**
4 large, ripe* **bananas**, halved lengthwise
1/4 cup **rum**
Confectioner's sugar

*If not ripe, gently squeeze the outside before peeling.

Preheat oven to 375°. Melt butter in saucepan. Add sugar and ginger, stirring to remove any lumps. Add orange and lemon juices, and simmer 10 minutes. Place bananas in shallow baking dish—avoid overlapping—and pour sauce over them. Bake 25 minutes or until slightly browned, basting once. Remove from oven, add the rum, and flame. Carefully transfer bananas to serving plates with spatula. Spoon pan sauce over top and sprinkle lightly with confectioner's sugar.

This recipe can also be done in a chafing dish. Always be very careful when applying the "pyrotechnics."

CREME CARAMEL

Serves 4

Caramel:
Butter
1/2 cup **white sugar**

Butter insides of 4 ramekins or dessert dishes. Melt sugar in heavy saucepan over medium heat. Shake the saucepan (do not stir) while sugar carmelizes. When sugar is completely liquid and dark brown, pour into ramekins.

Creme:
1 cup **heavy cream**
1 cup **milk**
2 **eggs**
2 **egg yolks**
1/2 cup **brown sugar**
2 teaspoons **cinnamon**
1/2 teaspoon **vanilla extract**
1/8 teaspoon **salt**
1 ounce **dark rum** *or* **brandy**

Scald cream and milk together. Meanwhile, mix well all remaining ingredients. Slowly combine with the scalded cream and milk mixture. Pour into ramekins. Place in pan of hot water and put in oven. Set heat to 300° and bake 1 hour or until custard is set. Cover and refrigerate overnight. To unmold, set ramekins in hot water for 10 seconds. Turn upside down onto serving dishes.

CREAMY CHEESE CAKE

Serves 8

Crust:
1 cup **graham-cracker** *or* **zwieback crumbs***
1/2 cup **butter** *or* **margarine**, melted
1/2 teaspoon **cinnamon**
  *Twelve finely crumbled graham crackers equal one cup.

Filling:
2 packages (8 oz.) **cream cheese**, softened
1/2 cup **sugar**
2 **eggs**
1 pint **sour cream**
1 teaspoon **vanilla extract**
2 teaspoons fresh **lemon juice**

Crust—Thoroughly combine crumbs, butter, and cinnamon. Spread evenly over bottom and sides of a 9" spring-form pan.

Filling—Beat together the cream cheese and sugar. Add eggs and mix well. Stir in sour cream, vanilla and lemon juice. Pour mixture into pan. Turn oven to 350° and bake for 45 minutes. When cool, cover and refrigerate at least 3 hours before serving.

A dessert supreme that is rarely served at home despite its easy preparation. For the sake of simplicity and purity of taste, such ingredients as grated lemon or orange peel and glazes have been eliminated.

CHILALA

Serves 4-6

3 cups **water**
1 stick **cinnamon**
1 package (3 oz.) **orange Jello**
1 package (3 oz.) **lemon Jello**
1 cup **medium-dry sherry**

Place water with cinnamon stick in saucepan and bring to boil.
Remove from heat and discard cinnamon stick. Add Jellos and
stir until completely dissolved. When Jello has cooled, add
sherry. Pour into mold and refrigerate until set. Serve with
whipped cream if desired.

A very simple dessert with a delightfully different taste.

CHEWY CHOCOLATE CHIP COOKIES
(Toll House Cookies)

**Makes about
4 dozen cookies**

2 sticks **butter**, softened
3/4 cup **granulated sugar**
1 cup **brown sugar**
2 **eggs**
1/2 teaspoon **vanilla extract**
1 3/4 cups **flour**, sifted
1/2 teaspoon **salt**
1 package (12 oz.) **semi-sweet chocolate chips**

Preheat oven to 325°. Beat butter until creamy. Gradually add both sugars making sure there are no lumps. Beat in eggs and vanilla. Sift in flour and salt, and beat vigorously. Add chocolate chips. Place teaspoonfuls of batter 3″ apart on cookie sheets—use aluminium or Teflon to reduce sticking. Bake 6 to 8 minutes or until lightly browned; allow 2 to 3 minutes before removing cookies with spatula.

Just-out-of-the-oven chocolate chip cookies accompanied by a tall glass of cold, fresh milk is tough to beat.

CHOCOLATE MOUSSE   Serves 6-8

8 ounces **semi-sweet chocolate**
3/4 cup **sugar**
2 teaspoons **instant coffee**
1 cup **water**
1/8 teaspoon **cream of tartar**
5 **egg whites**, at room temperature
3 **egg yolks**, beaten
1 pint **heavy cream**, whipped

Melt chocolate in double boiler over hot water. In a separate saucepan dissolve 1/2 cup sugar and coffee in water, and bring to boil. Combine well with chocolate and set aside to cool— 15 to 20 minutes. Meanwhile, add cream of tartar to egg whites and beat stiff but not dry, slowly adding remaining sugar. Blend egg yolks into cooled chocolate mixture. Then very gently but thoroughly fold in first the whipped cream and then the beaten egg whites. Turn into a chilled bowl or individual serving dishes and refrigerate at least 2 hours.

Alternatives: For a stronger **mocha** flavor simply increase the amount of coffee by 1 teaspoon. For a thicker consistency increase the number of egg yolks or decrease the number of egg whites.

This magnificence is so good it's ridiculous.

HOT CHOCOLATE PUDDING   Serves 4-6

3 tablespoons **butter**
2 squares **unsweetened chocolate**
1 cup **flour**
2 teaspoons **baking powder**
3/4 cup **white sugar**
1/4 teaspoon **salt**
1 cup **milk**
1 teaspoon **vanilla extract**
2 tablespoons **Kahlua** (optional)
1 cup **light brown sugar**
4 tablespoons **cocoa powder**
1 1/2 cups hot **water**

Grease 1 1/2-quart casserole with 1 tablespoon of the butter. In saucepan melt remaining butter and chocolate together over low heat. When melted, remove from heat and let cool. Meanwhile, sift together flour, baking powder, white sugar, and salt. Add milk, vanilla and cooled chocolate, and beat well. Pour batter into casserole. Sprinkle brown sugar and cocoa powder over batter. Pour Kahlua and water on top. Place in oven, turn heat to 350°, and bake 55 minutes.

From an old Boston recipe.

FRENCH CHOCOLATE SILK PIE   Serves 8

Crust:
1 1/4 cups **graham crackers** *or* **vanilla wafers**, crumbled
1 1/2 tablespoons **sugar**
6 tablespoons **butter**, melted

Preheat oven to 350°. In mixing bowl combine well all above ingredients. Line edge and bottom of 9" pie plate. Bake 7 minutes. (Crust can also be set without baking by simply chilling in refrigerator for 1 hour.)

Filling:
3/8 pound (1 1/2 sticks) **butter**, softened
1 cup and 2 tablespoons **superfine sugar**
1 1/2 squares **unsweetened chocolate**, melted
1 1/2 teaspoons **vanilla extract**
3 **eggs**
1/2 pint **whipping cream**
1 teaspoon **Grand Marnier**
1/4 cup **toasted almonds**, sliced (optional)

In mixing bowl beat butter until creamy; gradually stir in sugar and, beating constantly, add melted chocolate and vanilla. Add 2 eggs and beat 3 minutes. Add remaining egg and beat 3 more minutes. Pour mixture into cooled pie shell and refrigerate. Serve topped with whipped cream—whipped with Grand Marnier—and almonds.

Undoubtedly one of the finest pies I have ever tasted. This incomparable dessert was first experienced during a visit to one of the gourmet capitals of the world, New Orleans.

FAT FANNY'S FUDGE
FROM FLORIDA

**Yields about
1 1/2 pounds**

2 squares **unsweetened chocolate**, shaved
2 cups **sugar**
1 1/2 tablespoons **corn syrup** (optional)
3/4 cup **light cream**
1/2 teaspoon **salt**
2 tablespoons **butter**
1 teaspoon **vanilla extract**

In a heavy, medium-size saucepan, combine chocolate, sugar, corn syrup, cream, and salt. Place over low heat and stir until chocolate has melted. Bring to a boil over low heat and continue cooking—without stirring—until a drop of chocolate in cold water forms a soft ball—about 15 minutes. Remove from heat and place butter on top—do not stir. Let stand until lukewarm. Add vanilla and stir with wooden spoon until thick or until fudge just begins to lose its gloss. Lightly butter insides of small square pan and add fudge. Refrigerate to set—about 1/2 hour—and cut into squares.

The best anywhere! Maximum daily intake should be limited to 2 squares, otherwise there could be broadening consequences. A perfect companion to vanilla or coffee ice cream.

CINNAMON-ORANGE CAKE

**Makes one ring cake
or two loaf cakes**

3/4 cup **shortening**
1/2 cup **sugar**
2 **eggs**, separated
1/3 cup fresh **orange juice**
1 tablespoon grated **orange rind**
1/2 package **yellow cake mix**
1 teaspoon **baking soda**
1 teaspoon **cinnamon** or **allspice**
1 cup **sour cream**
1/4 teaspoon **cream of tartar**

Preheat oven to 350°. Cream shortening and sugar together.
Add egg yolks, juice, and rind and beat well. Sift together cake
mix, baking soda, and cinnamon. Stir into shortening mixture
alternately with sour cream. Beat egg whites and cream of tartar
together until stiff and fold into batter. Pour into well-greased
cake mold. Bake 45 minutes or until cake springs back after
gently pressing with finger. Let cake cool 10 minutes before
removing from pan.

HEATH N' HEAVEN

Serves 6-8

2 packages **Ladyfingers**
1 pint **heavy** or **whipping cream**
1/2 cup **confectioner's sugar**
8 **Heath bars**,* frozen

*Or any 1 ounce chocolate candy bar.

Line bottom and sides of 2-quart soufflé dish with Lady-fingers. Whip heavy cream, slowly adding sugar; beat until just stiff. Thoroughly pulverize frozen candy bars with wooden hammer or other appropriate implement. Mix cracked candy with whipped cream and turn into soufflé dish. Cover with plastic wrap and put in freezer to set—at least 2 hours.

Just about any chocolate candy bar can be substituted to make this delectable dessert.

HONEY CRUNCH   Serves 8

1/2 cup **honey**
1/4 cup **brown sugar**
1 1/2 tablespoons **butter**
1/4 teaspoon **salt**
5 1/2 cups **cornflakes**
1 quart **coffee** *or* **chocolate ice cream**

Place serving platter in freezer. Heat honey and brown sugar together in double boiler over boiling water. Stir in butter and salt breaking up any sugar lumps. Combine cornflakes with sauce. Turn into circular mold and refrigerate 1 hour. Place mold over chilled platter and demold by using a very hot damp towel. Serve with ice cream in the center of the mold.

Its simplicity belies its greatness.

LIMELITE
Serves 4

1 quart **lime ice** *or* **sherbet**

Sauce:
1 large **orange**, halved
1 **banana**, peeled and chopped
1 1/2 teaspoons **sugar** *or* **honey**
1/2 teaspoon **cinnamon** *or* **allspice**
2 teaspoons fresh **lime juice**
1 ounce **light rum** (optional)
1 tablespoon fresh **mint leaves**,* chopped

   *If available.

Place serving dishes in freezer for at least 30 minutes. From orange halves cut out sections of meat—avoid including any pulp. In small bowl thoroughly combine all ingredients for sauce and chill. When ready to serve, place scoops of lime ice or sherbet in each chilled dish and spoon sauce over each serving. Top with chopped mint leaves.

A perfect wrap-up to a summer meal.

EXTRA SPECIAL PECAN PIE   Serves 8

Single **9″ pie crust** (page 154)
3 **eggs**, slightly beaten
3/4 cup **light corn syrup**
1/4 cup each **dark brown** and **white sugar**
1/2 teaspoon **cinnamon**
2 tablespoons **butter**, melted
1 teaspoon **vanilla extract**
1/4 teaspoon **salt**
1 cup **pecans**

Preheat oven to 425°. Grease 9″ pie plate and fit with unbaked
pie dough. (Secure and flute dough around edge of pie plate as
desired.) Mix well all remaining ingredients except pecans,
breaking up any sugar lumps. Stir in pecans. Pour into pie shell.
Bake at 425° for 10 minutes, then 350° for 30 to 35 minutes, or
until filling has set.

Irresistible, incomparable, illegal. . . .

NEW AND EASY
PIE CRUST

Single crust for 8″ *or* 9″ pie
(double recipe to get 2 crusts)

2 tablespoons **butter**, softened
2 tablespoons **shortening**
3/4 cup **flour**
1/3 cup **sour cream**

Cut butter and shortening into flour until it becomes like bread crumbs. Add sour cream and work together. Form into a ball and refrigerate 1/2 hour (this makes dough easier to handle). On floured surface, press dough with flat bottom of pie plate or roll out to a circle 1″ larger than the pie plate. (This is easier if done between 2 pieces of wax paper.) Transfer pastry to well-greased pie plate and gently pat out any air pockets. With tines of fork, flute and trim pastry around rim. Then prick entire surface of pastry. To bake, place in 400° oven for 9 minutes or until lightly browned.

Not difficult and yields lots of pride.

GRANDMA'S RICE PUDDIN'   Serves 4

1/2 cup uncooked **white rice**
1 cup **water**
1/2 teaspoon **salt**
1 1/2 cup **whole milk**
3 tablespoons **sugar**
1/4 cup **raisins**
2 **eggs**, slightly beaten
1 teaspoon **vanilla extract**
1/4 teaspoon **ground cinnamon** or **nutmeg**

Combine rice, water and salt in heavy saucepan. Cook rice according to package directions—rice should be soft and fluffy. Stir in milk, sugar and raisins. Add eggs gradually and cook over low to medium heat, stirring constantly, until mixture is smooth and creamy. Remove from heat and stir in vanilla and cinnamon. Pour into ramekins and serve hot or cold—refrigerate 1 hour to chill.

Variation: substitute the raisins with chopped peaches, apricots, bananas, or apples

This old-time favorite is too often forgotten.

GRAND MARNIER SOUFFLÉ

Serves 4-6

1 tablespoon **butter**
2 tablespoons **powdered sugar**
6 **egg yolks**
1/2 cup **granulated sugar**
1 1/2 tablespoons grated **orange rind**
1/3 cup **Grand Marnier**
1/4 teaspoon **cream of tartar**
8 **egg whites**, at room temperature

Preheat oven to 425°. Butter bottom and sides of 2-quart soufflé dish. Sprinkle evenly with powdered sugar knocking out any excess. Beat yolks, adding sugar slowly until thick. Place over simmering water and heat, stirring constantly until hot and thick—around 10 minutes. Stir in orange rind and Grand Marnier. Put on ice to cool. Add cream of tartar to egg whites and beat until stiff. Stir one scoop of egg whites into cooled yolk mixture. Then slowly and gently fold remaining yolk mixture into egg whites. Turn into soufflé dish. Make a trench about 1" deep 1" from the edge all around the top. Place on middle shelf of oven and reduce heat to 400°. Bake for 25 minutes or until puffed high and nicely browned. Avoid opening oven door while soufflé is baking.

Total perfection...Serve with floradora sauce (page 122) to complete the coup.

PALMER'S ZABAGLIONE   Serves 4

4 **egg yolks**
1/2 cup **sugar**
3 ounces **medium-dry sherry**
2 **egg whites**

Put yolks, sugar, and sherry in double boiler and cook over
simmering water, stirring slowly and constantly. Just as it begins
to thicken (about 6 to 8 minutes), remove from heat and
continue to stir for 30 seconds. Beat egg whites until almost stiff.
Combine thoroughly with yolk mixture. Serve warm or chilled
according to season or preference.

*Plain, this dessert is incomparable. Served as a sauce with
strawberries, peaches or other fresh fruit, it is supreme.*

Appetizers and Snacks

Appetizers or hors d'oeuvres can be served as "cocktail food" or at the beginning of any full-course meal.

Snacks are small quantities of easily prepared, tasty foods which can be eaten at anytime, day or night.

GUACAMOLE

Yields about 3 cups

2 medium-size, ripe **avocados**, peeled, pitted and mashed
1 medium **tomato**, skinned and chopped
1 small **yellow onion**, finely chopped
1 1/2 tablespoons **hot chilies**, finely chopped
    or
1 teaspoon **chili powder**
1 tablespoon **olive oil**
2 teaspoons fresh **lime juice**
1 teaspoon fresh **lemon juice**
1 1/2 teaspoons **salt**
1/2 teaspoon **pepper**
3/4 teaspoon **coriander**

Combine all ingredients and stir into a textured paste. Serve chilled with warmed tortilla chips.

Add any of the following ingredients to the above recipe:

2 teaspoons fresh **parsley**, chopped
2 tablespoons crisp **bacon bits**
2 tablespoons **sour cream**
1/4 teaspoon **curry**
1/2 cup leftover **chicken** or **turkey meat**, minced

This Mexican favorite is best if made just before serving. However, if it is made ahead of time, be sure to put an avocado pit in the spread and cover tightly with cellophane wrap—this should help prevent the guacamole from discoloring.

MONIONS   Serves 6-8

6 slices **white bread**
3/4 cup **white onion**, finely chopped
5 tablespoons **mayonnaise**
Grated **Parmesan cheese**
Butter

Preheat oven to 350°. Using top of shot glass (1 3/4" wide) or
cookie cutter (1 1/2" wide), press out rounds from bread—usually
4 per slice. Combine well onion and mayonnaise, and mound on
bread rounds. Sprinkle lightly with Parmesan cheese and place
on buttered cookie sheets. Bake for 10 minutes or until browned
on top.

No big deal to prepare and always a big success.

PITTER-PÂTÉ

Yields two 3/4 lb. pâtés

1 envelope **Knox gelatin**
1 can (10 oz.) **beef bouillon**
6 ounces **liver pâté**
1 large (8 oz.) **Philadelphia cream cheese**

Dissolve gelatin in 1/4 cup bouillon. Heat remaining bouillon. Remove from heat and combine both bouillons. Pour 1/4" into two 3" dishes and refrigerate. While this gels, thoroughly mix the pâté and cream cheese with a fork. After gelatin solution has set, smooth pâté mixture on top. Add remaining gelatin solution and again refrigerate to set. Thirty minutes before serving, demold pâtés and let stand at room temperature. Serve with crackers.

THE WORLD'S GREATEST
RAW VEGETABLE DIP

Yields 3 cups

1 cup **sour cream**
1 jar (16 oz.) **mayonnaise**
2 1/2 tablespoons **lemon-pepper marinade**
1 tablespoon fresh **lemon** or **lime juice**
1 teaspoon **Dijon mustard**

Place all ingredients in bowl and combine thoroughly. Serve in chilled sauce bowl.

An extraordinary dip which goes very well with all fresh, raw, chilled vegetables served as appetizers. Some suggested vegetables are: asparagus, broccoli, carrots, cauliflower, celery, cucumber, radishes and scallions.

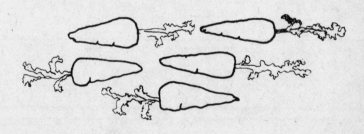

CHEESE DREAM

Serves 2

Butter
2 **English muffins**, halved (with fork rather than knife)
4 slices **tomato**
1 teaspoon **oregano**
Salt and **pepper** to taste
4 slices **American cheese**

Generously butter cut side of muffins and place on cookie sheet. Broil until they begin to brown. Place a tomato slice on each muffin and sprinkle with oregano, salt and pepper. Return to broiler for 3 minutes. Top with cheese and broil 2 more minutes or until cheese has melted and begins to brown.

This delicious variation of the grilled cheese sandwich retains a lot of heat after cooking, so take extra care not to burn yourself.

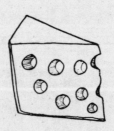

MONTANA BEEF JERKY   Yields about 2 1/2 pounds

3 pounds **lean beef**, cut 1/2" thick
3 tablespoons **salt**
3 tablespoons **coarse ground pepper**

Trim all fat from beef and cut lengthwise into 1/4" strips.
Sprinkle with salt and pepper. Press meat gently to insure
seasoning will adhere. Hang in bright, warm sun, or place on
racks in a 150° oven with the door slightly open for 6 or 7 hours.
Store refrigerated in an airtight container.

*A big favorite as a high energy, tasty snack. Remember it for
your next hunting, fishing or camping trip. Jerky is derived from
the Spanish word charqui, meaning dried beef.*

MUSHROOMS A LA DAUM   Serves 2

1 cup fresh **mushrooms**, sliced
1/2 cup **yellow onions**, minced
1/2 cup **ham**, chopped
1 teaspoon **fresh parsley**, minced
1/4 teaspoon **salt**
1/8 teaspoon **pepper**
4 tablespoons **butter**
1/2 cup **brown gravy**
2 slices **white bread**, toasted

Combine mushrooms, onions, ham and seasoning, and saute in butter for about 12 minutes over a medium flame. Stir in gravy and serve on toast.

A quick and easy delight from the hallowed halls of "21."

SWEET N' SOUR PICKLES

1 gallon **sour pickles**, cut into 1" slices
Ice
3 pounds **sugar**
6 cloves **garlic**
1 small package mixed **pickling spices**
1 quart **tarragon vinegar**

Place pickles in large crock and cover with ice for 30 minutes; drain. Return pickles to jar, layering with sugar, garlic and spices. Add vinegar. Put top on loosely and let stand 5 days at room temperature, stirring each day. Store refrigerated in jar with top on.

This family recipe comes from the great "nation" of Texas.

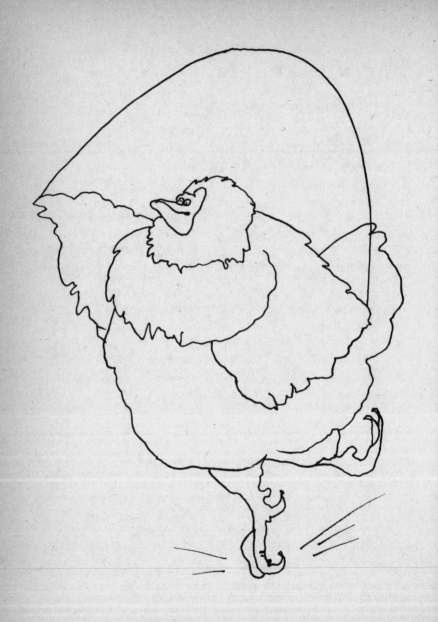

Drinks

PORTER: ". . . Drink sir, is a great provoker of three things. . . nose-painting, sleep and urine. Lechery, sir, it provokes and unprovokes; it provokes the desire, but it takes away the performance. . ."

Act II, Macbeth
Shakespeare

BLOODY BULL

**Makes 2
10 oz. drinks**

1 cup **tomato** or **V-8 juice**
1 cup **beef bouillon**
4 ounces **vodka***
2 teaspoons **Worcestershire sauce**
1/4 cup fresh **lemon juice**
4 drops **Tabasco sauce**
1/2 teaspoon **celery salt**
1/4 teaspoon **pepper**

*Tequila or gin are excellent substitutes.

Put all ingredients over ice in cocktail shaker and stir. Serve on or off the rocks.

Alternatives:

BLOODY BULL minus:

bouillon = Bloody Mary
tomato juice = Bull Shot
vodka and bouillon = Virgin Mary
vodka and tomato juice = Sterile Bull

If you wake up with a crashing hangover, go back to sleep—it is by far and away the best cure. Later on to ease any lingering pain, any of the above are suggested.

FRESH FRUIT DAIQUIRI **Makes 4 drinks**

2 cups of any of the following **fresh fruit:**
banana   peaches
melon   strawberries
1/4 cup fresh **lime juice**
4 tablespoons **sugar**
1 **egg white**
6 ounces **light rum**
2 or 3 cups **ice**

Place all ingredients in blender and mix at high speed for 40 seconds.

A warm weather smash hit.

HOLIDAY EGG NOG

**Makes 10
8 oz. drinks**

6 **egg yolks**
1/4 cup **sugar**
2 cups **bourbon**
1 quart **Half & Half**
1/2 teaspoon grated **nutmeg**
6 **egg whites**
1 ounce **cognac** (optional)

Beat egg yolks. Add sugar and continue to beat until thick. Slowly mix in bourbon and Half & Half. Add nutmeg. In separate bowl beat egg whites until almost stiff. Fold into yolk mixture. Add cognac. Refrigerate about 2 hours before serving. Sprinkle a small amount of nutmeg over each serving.

A magnificent concoction which is perfect for winter's festive gatherings.

FARMER'S BISHOP

**Makes about 20
8 oz. drinks**

1 gallon **apple cider**
4 **cinnamon sticks**
24 **cloves**
4 **oranges**
1 cup **Calvados** *or* **brandy**
1 quart **apple jack** *or* **bourbon**

Heat cider with cinnamon sticks in large pot—do not boil.
Meanwhile, stick 6 cloves in each orange and bake them whole
at 300° for 1 hour. Then halve the oranges and put them in
another pot squeezing some juice from each half. Separately,
heat the Calvados—do not boil—light it, and pour over oranges.
Let burn 5 seconds, then extinguish flame by adding the hot
cider. Add apple jack and heat to serving temperature—do not
boil.

*Absolute perfection for a bunch of people on a cold winter's
night.*

THE ORIGINAL IRISH COFFEE   **Yields 2 drinks**

8 ounces (1 cup) fresh **black coffee**
3 ounces **Irish whiskey**
2 teaspoons **sugar**
1/2 cup **heavy cream**, lightly whipped

Preheat glasses with hot water—discard water. Put coffee, Irish whiskey and sugar into glasses and stir. Top with whipped cream and serve.

A cold-weather treat.

GLÜWEIN
(Mulled Wine)

**Makes 8
8 oz. drinks**

1/2 gallon **red burgundy**
1/2 cup **brandy**
1/2 cup **honey**
1 **orange peel**
2 **cinnamon sticks**

Combine all ingredients and slowly heat to just before boiling—do not allow to boil. Serve in mugs.

A guaranteed warmer during or after activities on cold winter days or nights.

KIR   **Makes 2 drinks**

4 drops **cassis**
8 ounces **dry white wine**, chilled

Place two drops of cassis in each wine glass and add wine. Serve with or without ice as preferred.

This drink is properly made very dry, i.e., a small amount of cassis. The French accomplish this by swirling a 1/2 ounce of cassis in the glass, pouring it all out—or back in the bottle—and then adding the wine.

LIME RICKEY   **Makes 2 drinks**

4 ounces fresh **lime juice***
3 ounces **rum, gin,** *or* **vodka**
2 teaspoons **sugar**
Soda water

*Approximately 3 medium limes.

Put lime juice and sugar in glasses and stir to dissolve sugar.
Add liquor and fill glasses with ice. Top off with soda water, stir
and serve.

*If you like the taste of lime, this drink has it big: a perfect
summer cooler.*

PIÑA COLADA

Makes 2 drinks

4 ounces **cream of coconut**
4 ounces **light rum**
8 ounces **unsweetened pineapple juice**
1 cup crushed **ice**

Place all ingredients in electric blender and mix for about
20 seconds. Serve on or off the rocks as preferred.

An ideal blend of tropical ambrosias.

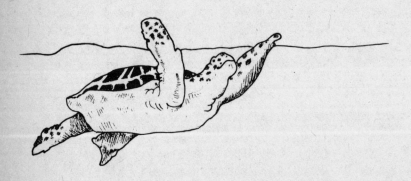

SPRITZER
Makes 2 drinks

8 ounces **dry white wine**
Soda water
2 **lemon peels**

Pour wine over ice, add soda water and stir gently. Twist and drop lemon peel into each drink.

A curiously refreshing drink which makes a little bit of wine go a lot farther.

HOT BUTTERED RUM
Makes 2 drinks

2 teaspoons **butter**
4 ounces **rum** (light, amber, or Anejo)
2 **lemon peels**
2 teaspoons **honey**
2 **cinnamon sticks**
Boiling **water**

Divide first 5 ingredients between two glasses. Put a spoon in each glass* and add enough boiling water to fill. Stir and serve.

If it's cold, this will warm it up in a hurry.

*Placing a spoon in a glass to which boiling water is being added tempers the heat of the water and prevents the glass from breaking.

WASHBURN

1 daiquiri + 1 iced tea = 1 Washburn

4 sprigs fresh **mint**
Ice cubes
1/2 cup fresh **lemon juice**
2 cups **iced tea**, homemade *or* instant
2 tablespoons **sugar**

Put leaves from 2 mint sprigs and ice cubes in cocktail shaker and shake briefly to "bruise" mint. Add remaining ingredients and shake well. Serve in chilled glasses with a sprig of mint in each drink.

A warm weather libation which is fully guaranteed to put a cool on the heat.

DRINKS
(non-alcoholic)

PALMER'S INSTANT ICED TEA

**Yields about
2 quarts**

4 packs (2-oz. size) **instant iced tea mix**
2 quarts **water**
3/4 cup fresh **orange juice**
1/4 cup fresh **lemon juice**
4 sprigs fresh **mint**

Combine all ingredients in large pitcher and stir well. Refrigerate 2 to 3 hours to chill and to allow mint to flavor tea.

To give this drink some sparkle, try adding 1 quart ginger ale.

If preferred, use your own homebrewed tea in this recipe. Using packages of instant tea makes preparation simpler and faster.

COFFEE

An average of 450,000,000 cups of coffee are consumed in the USA every day.

COFFEEMAKER	TIME	GRIND
Vacuum	1-4 mins.	Fine or vacuum
Drip	4-6 mins.	Drip
Regular or percolator	6-8 mins.	Regular

1. Choose the proper grind for your particular coffeemaker.

2. Always start with a clean coffeemaker and cold water.

3. Most coffeemakers work best when used to at least three-quarters of their capacity. Therefore, it may be helpful to have two sizes—one for every day, one for company.

4. Exact proportions of coffee to water will produce a better cup of coffee. All coffeemakers require the same proportions per cup of coffee:

   2 level tablespoons coffee to 6 ozs. (three-quarters of a cup) water.

For a weaker brew, hot water should be added *after* the coffee has been made at full strength.

5. For best results, different grinds should be brewed for the right length of time.

6. The fresher the grind, the better the brew. Coffee does not keep well after exposure to air. However, freshness can be maintained longer if ground coffee is refrigerated—freezing is even better—in a sealed container. (Freeze-dried coffee does not require refrigeration.)

7. For fresher flavor, coffee should always be served as soon as possible after brewing. Brewed coffee should *never* be allowed to boil—boiling destroys flavor. To keep coffee warm use a metal

"flame tamer" over a low flame, an electric trivet, or a *bain Marie* (a "bath" of simmering water).

8. Adding salt to coffee grinds does nothing to enhance the quality or taste of brewed coffee.

9. A dash—less than 1/8 teaspoon—of cinnamon, cardamom, or allspice in the grinds before brewing will add flavor to coffee. Experimentation will establish preference and exact measurements of condiments.

10. For demitasse service simply reduce the amount of water by half, i.e., 3 ozs., instead of 6 ozs., of water per 2 tablespoons of coffee.

Appendix

CULINARY CUES

Any and all information which can help produce better results in the kitchen is always welcome.

CULINARY CUES:

A

Avocado: Discoloration of an avocado dip can be prevented by placing an avocado pit into the dip then covering and refrigerating before serving.

B

Bacon: Stripping bacon from a cold slab of presliced bacon is made easier if, before opening, the package is rolled tightly and released; this should make the slices separate with less trouble.

A simple alternative to pan-frying bacon is to bake it in a shallow baking pan lined with foil at 325° for 30 to 35 minutes. This eliminates the need to flip or tend the bacon, and it turns out dry and crisp after draining on absorbent paper.

Baking: Glass dishes and shiny metal pans require 25° less heat for baking than pans with a dull finish.

Beef: Large steaks or roasts which have been grilled, roasted, broiled, or pan-broiled should be allowed to stand, covered, for 10 to 15 minutes before carving. This lets the juices distribute evenly through the meat.

Beets: Red beets keep their color if a few teaspoons of vinegar are added to the cooking water.

Bread: A degree of freshness can be restored to stale bread by the following: spread butter lightly on one side of each slice. Return bread to original package and place in a warm oven (150°) for 15 minutes.

Brown sugar: After opening, brown sugar should be stored in an airtight container to prevent it from drying out and hardening.

Butter: An equivalent amount of margarine can be substituted for purposes of controlling cholesterol intake. It should be noted, however, that there is little difference in calories between the two.

Clarified — Butter is clarified in order to remove additives which burn and smoke at high temperatures. To clarify butter, simply heat at a low temperature until the impurities have separated and settled, then pour off the clear fat taking care not to include any residue. (Butter can be stabilized for cooking at moderate temperatures by adding oil in a ratio of 4 to 1, butter to oil.)

Sweet butter — This butter has a fresher taste than salted butter, and therefore makes it preferable for baking. However, as it contains no additives or preservatives, it can turn rancid and tends to burn at lower temperatures.

C

Cakes: To prevent cakes from sticking to baking tins, grease insides with butter and sprinkle with flour and/or confectioner's sugar—shake off any excess.

Canned foods: Avoid leaving food in tin cans after opening, even under refrigeration. Oxidation of the metal container can cause harmful contamination of the food.

Cauliflower: A tablespoon of lemon juice or vinegar in the cooking water will keep the vegetable whiter.

Citrus fruit: A little juice from a lemon, lime, or orange will not only enhance the taste of sliced fruit such as apples, peaches and pears, but will also keep the fruit from discoloring.

Cream: Natural heavy cream has a shelf-life of about 10 days under refrigeration. However, a new sterilizing process has been introduced to increase shelf-life to 6 weeks. Unfortunately, the process results in a loss in both taste and "whipability." To solve the latter problem, put some ice cubes in a large bowl and cover them with water. Put the cream in a copper pan, set it in the ice water and whip.

To make sour cream, add 1 teaspoon vinegar or lemon juice to 1 cup heavy cream, and let stand 5 minutes.

D

Defrosting: It is better to allow food to defrost slowly in the refrigerator rather than at room temperature. Defrost duck, chicken, pheasant and all other fowl—domestic or wild—in cold milk. This tenderizes the meat and heightens the flavor.

E

Eggs: To test the freshness of an egg, drop it in a bowl of water: the less buoyant it is, the fresher it is.

It is easier to separate an egg if it is cold.

Whites — For best results when beating egg whites:
1 — use a copper bowl
2 — all equipment should be washed
3 — egg whites should be at room temperature
4 — adding a dash of cream of tartar before beating will help hold volume.

Yolks — Traditionally yolks have been used in sauces to add consistency and texture. However, due to publicity regarding their high cholesterol content, alternatives such as arrowroot, flour, and cornstarch are gaining preference.

F

Flour: All flour and flour mixtures (for pancakes, biscuits, etc.) should be stored in sealed containers to prevent infestation by bugs and their larvae.

To prevent flour from caking when added to sauces, stews, etc., simply combine with a small amount of cold water to make a smooth paste.

To make 1 cup self-rising flour, combine 1 cup flour, 1/4 teaspoon salt and 2 teaspoons baking powder.

G

Garlic: Peeling garlic is simplified if the stem is pressed into a hard surface which will free the peel from the stem.

H

Herbs: Many herbs begin to lose their potency after four months. Always store them in airtight containers.

I

Ice cream: If stored in a freezer for more than one month, ice cream can begin to crystallize and separate thereby losing texture and flavor.

L

Lemons: They will yield more juice at room temperature than if chilled.

Add lemon after fish has been cooked, never before.

Lemon or lime juice will remove fruit stains from skin.

Lettuce: To separate the stem from a head of lettuce without a knife, give the stem one or two sharp blows with the heal of your hand and then with a twisting-pulling action, detach the stem from the leaves.

M

Melon: Serve slightly chilled or at room temperature, as excessive chilling tends to inhibit taste.

Mushrooms: After slicing, rinse mushrooms in a solution of 1 part lemon juice to 4 parts cold water; this will reduce discoloring and keep them fresher.

O

Oils: Avoid getting oils so hot that they smoke; over-heated oil can spoil the taste of food and cause indigestion.

Olive oil — Putting a small cube of sugar in olive oil will help prevent it from turning rancid.

Onions: Types — Bermuda, Spanish, or red
garlic
leeks
scallions
shallots
white or pearl
yellow or globe

Crying — Chilling any member of the onion family before slicing will reduce, if not eliminate, tearing.

Odor — Wash hands with vinegar or lemon juice to remove traces of onion smell.

Orange juice: A quick trip in a blender for orange juice out of a can or carton does much to improve flavor.

P

Parsley (fresh): If kept in a dry, airtight plastic bag or jar, and refrigerated, parsley will stay fresh for about two weeks.

Plates: Hot food should always be served on warmed plates. Warming plates takes little time and effort, and can be done in several ways:
   1—place in 175° oven for about 8 minutes
   2—place in hot water for 5 minutes and dry
   3—place on hot tray until warm

Poaching: *Eggs* — The whites of eggs will hold together better when being poached if the egg is rolled in boiling water for 5-10 seconds before breaking and/or 1 teaspoon vinegar is added to the poaching water.

Fruit — Always use enamel, glass, or pottery saucepans when poaching light-colored fruits; metal pans tend to discolor the fruit.

Potatoes: Do not confuse baking potatoes with boiling potatoes. In general, the shape of a baking or old potato is more oblong than a boiling or new potato.

S

Salad dressing: Always mix seasoning with vinegar before adding oil. At meals where good vintage wines are being served, it is best to substitute lemon juice for vinegar in salad dressings (on a ratio of 1 for 2) as vinegar will temporarily overpower taste buds and therefore detract from the full appreciation of the wine.

Sesame seeds: Add a dash of salt to pan when roasting sesame seeds to prevent sticking, and always use a low heat.

Steaming: A colander placed over boiling water and covered is a good substitute for steaming vegetables if the proper equipment is not available.

APPENDIX

T

Tabasco sauce: Always keep refrigerated after opening. The color of the sauce should approximate the bright red color of the bottle cap.

Tomatoes: They can be peeled easily if submerged in boiling water for 20 seconds.

V

Vegetables: Rules of thumb:
  If it grows beneath the ground, place in cold salted water, cover, and bring to a boil. Continue to boil until fork tender.
  If it grows above the ground, place in rapidly boiling salted water and cook, uncovered, until just fork tender. (The trick to keeping the color and fresh taste in green vegetables is to get them as cold as possible—without freezing—before putting them in boiling water.)

W

Wine (white): Chill by refrigerating at least one hour before drinking. When using an ice bucket, allow 25 minutes, turning the bottle occasionally.

CHEESE, FRUIT AND WINE

Cheese and fruit most definitely go together. As a dessert, combinations of fruit and cheese are not only elegant but delicious. The fruit and beverage chosen for a meal should be used as guidelines for selecting the appropriate cheese or cheeses. The following chart should be of assistance in making selections in all three categories. Of course, with experimentation different combinations will be discovered. A rule of thumb to remember in combining wines and cheeses is to match them by strength or intensity of flavor: light, delicate wines with delicate cheeses, etc.

For a luncheon with a European touch, try some cheese and fruit combinations with French bread and a bottle of whatever wine suits the taste.

CHEESE, FRUIT, AND BEVERAGE CHART

Cheeses (soft to semi-soft)	Fruit	Beverage
Appenzeller	white grapes red plums	dry white wine cider
Beaumont	apples pears	dry white wine cider
Bel Paese	apples pears	dry white wine cider
Brie	apples pears nectarines	white wine (Mosel and Rhine) champagne
Camembert	grapes pears pineapples	white wine (Muscadet) champagne
Coeur de Neufchatel	apples pears	white wine (Muscadet)
Crema Danica	apples Bing cherries grapes	medium-dry white wine cider
Feta	red grapes	dry white wine
Port-l'Eveque	apples pears white grapes	white wine (Muscadet) dry cider
Provolone	pears red grapes	dry white wine cider
Vacherin	red plums white grapes	dry white wine cider

Cheeses (semi-hard to hard)	Fruit	Beverage
Danablu	apples	lager beer
Edam	honeydew melon	beer
Gorgonzola	peaches	red wine (Barolo)
Parmesan	apples cantaloupe	semi-sweet white wine
Roquefort	apples grapes oranges pears	red wine (Burgundy) sauterne
Samø	honeydew melon	red wine (Burgundy)
Stilton	figs plums	port or sherry

FRUIT CHART

APPLES:* Baldwin — rare, sweet-sour
     Cortland — tart, great for pie
     Golden Delicious — dry and sweet, good for tarts and
               fried apple rings
     Granny Smith — piquant
     Green Newton Pippin — scarce, sharp, good for pie or eating
     Jonathan — mildly spicy
     Macoun — deliciously pungent
     McIntosh — good eating, great for applesauce
     Northern Spy — bittersweet, juicy
     Red Delicious — crisp, sweet
     Rhode Island Greening — perfect for sour pie
     Rome Beauty — mild-flavored, good for baking
     Stayman — like Winesap, only more so
     Winesap — rare, cinnamon-scented and tart
     York Imperial — scarce, winy, good for baking

    *This information on apples came from an article in New York Magazine
    called "Hard Core Pomology."

APRICOTS	PEARS
BANANAS	PERSIMMONS
BLACKBERRIES	PINEAPPLE
BLUEBERRIES	PLUMS
CHERRIES	PRUNES
FIGS	ORANGES
GRAPEFRUIT	RAISINS
GRAPES: Catawba	RASPBERRIES
Concord	STRAWBERRIES
Seedless White	TANGERINES
MANGOES	
MELON: Cantaloupe	
Casaba	
Crenshaw	
Honeydew	
Persian	
Watermelon	
NECTARINES	
PAPAYAS	
PEACHES	

COMMON WEIGHTS AND MEASURES*

It is best never to add ingredients without measuring. Only after a great deal of experience should one try "eye measurements." Also, avoid measuring over food in preparation as there is always the chance of a loose cap or top falling off or some such mishap which could ruin a dish.

VOLUME EQUIVALENTS

dash	less than 1/8 teaspoon	1 milliliter
1 teaspoon	1/3 tablespoon	5 milliliters
3 teaspoons	1 tablespoon	15 milliliters
2 tablespoons	1 fluid ounce	30 milliliters
4 tablespoons	1/4 cup	60 milliliters
8 tablespoons	1/2 cup	120 milliliters
1 cup	8 ounces	240 milliliters
2 cups	1 pint	480 milliliters
4 cups	1 quart	960 milliliters
4 quarts	1 gallon	3.84 liters

WEIGHT EQUIVALENTS

common package
or can sizes

1 ounce		28 grams
6 ounces	3/4 cup	168 grams
8 ounces	1 cup	224 grams
No. 1 (11 ounces)	1 1/3 cups	308 grams
No. 303		
(16 ounces)	2 cups (1 pound)	448 grams
No. 2 (20 ounces)	2 1/2 cups	560 grams
No. 2 1/2		
(28 ounces)	3 1/2 cups	784 grams

To convert milliliters into liters, divide by 1000
example: 120 milliliters ÷1000 = 12 liters

To convert kilograms into grams, multiply by 1000
example: .22 kilograms × 1000 = 220 grams

*The metric system is expected to be fully adopted as the national standard of weights and measures sometime between 1980 and 1985.

OVEN CHART

Warming	175 - 250°*
Very slow	250 - 275°
Slow (or low)	300 - 325°
Moderate	350 - 375°
High (or hot)	400 - 425°
Very high	450 - 475°
Extremely high	500 - 525°

*Fahrenheit.

One of the most important aspects of successful cooking is knowledge of the range which will be roasting, broiling, or baking your food. Ovens can be temperamental, producing either too much or too little heat. Wide variations from a specified cooking temperature can understandably result in total failure; this is especially true for breads and soufflés for which an exact amount of heat for the right amount of time is critical to their success.

It is wise to have your oven checked by an expert once a year to ensure that temperature gauges are correct and in proper working order. On your own you can check the accuracy of your oven every three or four months with an oven thermometer. Such testing will also familiarize you with the amount of time required to heat your oven to various temperatures which is helpful information for timing the preparation of meals.

When baking, check to see whether the heat source of the oven is electric (direct or exposed) or gas (indirect or chambered). If direct, be sure to place the cooking implement either on a cookie sheet or in a shallow pan of hot water; this will prevent the possibility of scorching.

Quite obviously a major portion of the guesswork in cooking will be eliminated if you can be assured of the accuracy of your oven and, consequently, your own chances of cooking successfully will be greatly improved.

ACKNOWLEDGMENTS

My sources for this book were many and varied. The recipes, whether standards or "originals," came from friends, their friends, relatives, domestics, restaurants, and my personal cache. In cases where I was refused knowledge of a particularly good recipe, I guessed the ingredients and preparation and tested until I reproduced the original dish as closely as possible.

Whatever or whoever the source, I want to extend my thanks to all who advised, contributed, tested, and encouraged, and hope that justice was done in presentation.

Index

INDEX

INDEX

INDEX

INDEX